the glorious world of golf

Special Material. THE NEW Warranted Well Seasoned.

a ridge press book ☼ mcgraw-hill boo[k]

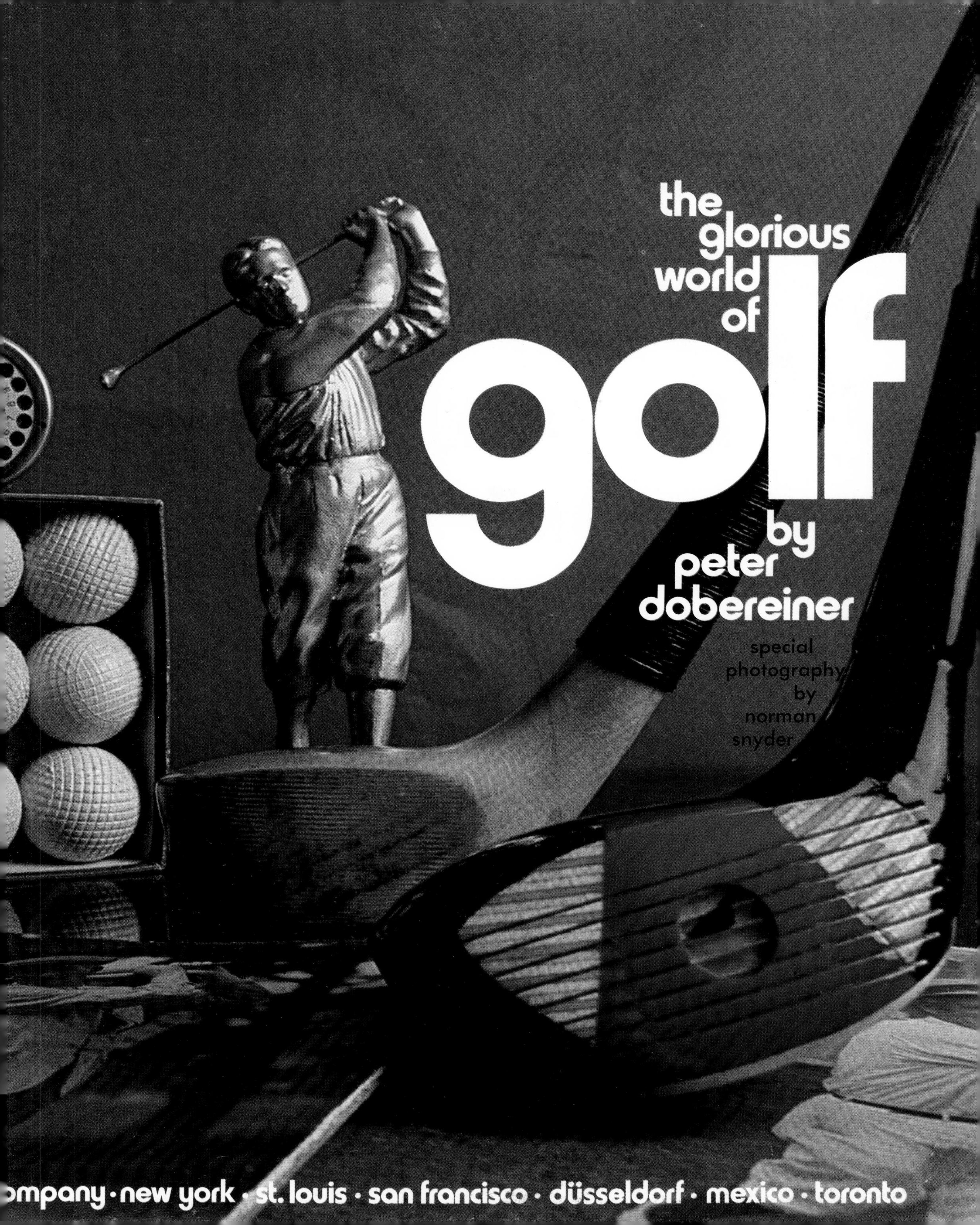

the
glorious
world
of
golf

by
peter
dobereiner

special
photography
by
norman
snyder

ompany · new york · st. louis · san francisco · düsseldorf · mexico · toronto

Editor-in-Chief: Jerry Mason
Editor: Adolph Suehsdorf
Art Director: Albert Squillace
Project Art Director: Harry Brocke
Associate Editor: Moira Duggan
Associate Editor: Barbara Hoffbeck
Art Associate: Mark Liebergall
Art Associate: David Namias
Art Production: Doris Mullane
Picture Research: Marion Geisinger

Prepared and produced by The Ridge Press, Inc.
Published by the McGraw-Hill Book Company, New York.
Library of Congress Catalog Card Number: 73-75615
ISBN: 07-017150-5
Printed and bound in Italy by Mondadori Editore, Verona.

For the golfing orphans, Jane and Ruth

contents

foreword

The Basset hound is a foolish dog and mine is a particularly stupid example of the breed. As I write she is crouched in the far corner of my study staring at me in suspicion with watery, bloodshot eyes. Already I can see by her furrowed brow that she thinks she has seen me before but can't quite place the face. When the moment of recognition dawns she will explode into violent activity and go tearing around the house knocking over small pieces of furniture in elephantine ecstasy and baying fit to wake the dead. A mile away across the valley the people in the village will know that I am home.

By now I have come to accept the experience of being snubbed by my own dog as an occupational hazard. In two weeks we will have another of these strained reunions. And so it will go on all year. The life of a professional golf writer seems to me in my blacker moments to be spent entirely in airport lounges listening to announcements to the effect that his flight has been delayed yet another five hours. I calculate that in one year I fly 70,000 miles, drive 20,000, and cover 10,000 miles by train. That's just getting to golf courses. Once there I walk a distance equivalent to hiking from New York to Waco, Texas, just watching other people play golf.

There is a truism in this business that the professional golf watcher never catches the action. I could write a volume on Great Moments in Golf I Have Missed. When Tommy Bolt hurled his wedge into the lake (well, one of the times anyway) I was two fairways away. When Arnold Palmer hit his shot-of-the-century at Royal Birkdale I was temporarily absent in the men's room. And at the time Brian Barnes was taking fifteen strokes on a par-3 in the French Open I was covering an amateur tournament in a different country.

With a game like golf that kind of thing is inevitable. Even so, I have seen many strange and wonderful events. And, perhaps even more rewarding, I have talked with many strange and wonderful people. In Portugal, respectfully seated at the feet of the Master, I have listened to Henry Cotton expound on the virtues of a dominant right hand in the golf stroke. In Florida I have dutifully recorded Lee Trevino's dissertation on the need for a dominant left hand. And in Melbourne I have sat with notebook agog as Peter Thomson demolished both theories with a sardonic laugh.

These, then, are my credentials for writing this book. I do not speak with the authority of a great player. What small facility I once had for the game has long since been lost in the turbulence of jet travel and the lack of playing opportunities. But I think I can truthfully claim that my enthusiasm for golf has not dimmed with overexposure.

Possibly I no longer thrill to a shot which pitches a yard past the flag, takes one bounce, and then screws back to the hole. The galleries go wild with delight, but now that I have analyzed the mechanics of such shots with a hundred different professionals my sense of wonder is attuned to subtler aspects of the game.

Although this book is not a history of golf, a certain proportion of it is devoted to the past because I feel this to be important. Let us take the analogy of a gourmet in a Chinese restaurant. Would he enjoy his egg more if he knew that it had been set aside specially for his delight a hundred years previously? I think he would. And I believe that those of us who play golf get a similarly enhanced pleasure from knowing something about the traditions and history of golf, and about some of the early exponents of the game, and about how the other half of the golfing world lives.

My life in golf has been a rewarding experience. My hope is that some of that pleasure will rub off onto anyone who may read this book. If it gives enjoyment in the reading, or if its afterglow heightens the enjoyment of playing the game, then it will have served its purpose.

April, 1973   Peter Dobereiner

1 · the loneliest game

What is golf? The question is easier asked than answered. Golf defies definition, although plenty of good men have tried. Arthur Balfour wrote, with the pomposity befitting a statesman: "A tolerable day, a tolerable green and a tolerable opponent supply—or ought to supply—all that any reasonably constituted human being should require in the way of entertainment."

On close examination that statement tells us more about politics than golf. Look at the care with which the words have been chosen to provide escape clauses. It might have been framed to resist attack by the militants of the Anti-Golf Party.

"Is the Prime Minister claiming golf to be the perfect form of entertainment?"

"No, sir! If the honorable gentleman will study my statement, he will notice the reference to 'reasonably constituted human beings.' I would not recommend golf to members of the Opposition."

Laughter, jeers, and cries of "Withdraw."

"Does the Prime Minister mean that for reasonably constituted human beings *like himself* golf is all the entertainment they ever require?"

"Again I would draw the honorable gentleman's attention to what I actually said. I have never suggested that in all circumstances. . . ."

And so on. Strip the qualifications from Balfour's definition and you are left with the insipid message that people who enjoy golf are occasionally happy to play. What profundity!

Bobby Jones, who wrote about golf almost as well as he played it, never attempted a definition. The nearest he came to encapsulating golf was in occasional reflective asides on aspects of the game, such as, "Golf, in my view, is the most rewarding of all games because it possesses a very definite value as a molder or developer of character. The golfer very soon is made to realize that his most immediate, and perhaps his most potent, adversary is himself." The

wisdom of this remark will quickly become obvious to anyone who takes up the game. It will do for a start.

Let us try a writer. A. A. Milne put it: "Golf is popular simply because it is the best game in the world at which to be bad." Now we are getting somewhere. Here is a bone on which we can chew, plus a meaty morsel of paradox. It is obviously true that in the army of golf the majority of players are humble private soldiers, the happy hackers, while the noncommissioned officers and the brass, the scratch golfers and lordly professionals, are serious fellows for whom golf provides more satisfaction than fun.

There comes a stage in the progress of a golfer which is the equivalent to winning his stripes. At this point he ceases to savor the good shots and starts instead to grieve over the bad ones. The hacker expects to hit bad shots. They are his natural stock-in-trade. Consequently, when he does fire off the rare winner, with the ball coming flush off the clubface and flying straight at the target, he experiences a glow of satisfaction which is positively sensual. He can savor the delicious memory of that one shot for a week.

For the good golfer such shots are normal. The ball flies straight(ish) and true(ish) most of the time. Some are better than others, but for him the exceptional emotion is disappointment. After a round, the scratch man kicks the door of his locker and curses the hooked drive into a pond which cost him a 6. The 24 handicapper comes in almost incandescent from the afterglow of that five-iron to the short hole which finished six feet from the flag. Never mind that he three-putted—that is beside the point.

How did the scratch man play that particular hole? "You mean the seventh? Oh, yes. Seven-iron and then my ten-footer lipped out. How they expect you to hole a putt on these damned greens, I don't know. I've told them a thousand times to lower the cutters to five thirty-seconds and cross-mow against the grain."

Preceding pages: Blast! Golfer suits his action to the word at Hilton Head, South Carolina. For once, the violent banging of a club into the ground may release trapped ball as well as emotions.

Yes, the privates are the happy ones. Or are they? What wouldn't that hacker give to hit the 7th green with a seven-iron as a matter of routine. You name it—anything.

If the legend of Dr. Faustus were applied to golf we would quickly get to the truth about the game. The Devil offers a deal. In return for the deed to your house, your handicap comes down by four shots; exchange your bank balance for another four shots; throw in your wife and you can be scratch. . . . There would soon be a dramatic improvement in golfing standards—played by morose, divorced paupers. As with Wellington's army, every golfing private carries a field marshal's baton in his golf bag.

Perhaps the historian, Sir Walter Simpson, was nearer the truth with his bleak statement that "excessive golf dwarfs the intellect." Certainly, golf makes idiots of us all at times. However, let us take refuge in that word "excessive," since excess in anything is harmful. Simpson was writing in the context of match play and suggesting that it was prudent to bet on the dull-eyed fellow who did not have the wit or imagination to feel the destructive psychological pressures of golf.

There is a grain of truth in that idea. Certainly, many a golfer has been destroyed more by his own sensitivity than by the course or his opponent. But it is a matter of simple observation that the very best players are highly intelligent men who recognize the demons conjured up in their own imagination and face them squarely for what they are. The unimaginative clot with a sound method can make a good golfer, but it takes brains to make a great one.

You might think that the obvious place to find a satisfactory answer to our question, "What is golf?" could be found in the rules of the game. The laws are so complex that of the world's forty million players there are probably fewer than one hundred with a comprehensive knowledge of all the tangled legal ramifications. What other game comes to a complete halt while experienced professionals send for expert advice as to the correct procedure for them to follow? However, Rule 1, which is the nearest thing you can get to an official definition of golf, is relatively straightforward: "The game consists in playing a ball from the teeing ground into the hole by successive strokes in accordance with the rules. Penalty for breach of rule: Match play, loss of hole; stroke play, disqualification."

That flat statement, which has a certain elegance in its extremes of banality, does not get us far. It does raise the intriguing question of how you can possibly break this rule. In the preamble to the rules we are told: "Every word means what it says." That's clear enough.

There must be a reason for the rule, because it did not appear in the early codes of the game. At some time it became necessary for the legislators of the game to frame this law to the effect that the first rule of golf is that the game must be played according to the rules. And this is followed by a glorious rule giving a scale of penalties in cases where the lawmakers have not made any rules.

No wonder golfers are not too well versed in the rules. However, in the wider sense of our question, "What is golf?" the rules do supply one clue, albeit a false one. That first rule is headed "The Game." And one point on which all golfers can immediately agree is that, whatever else golf may be, it is not a game. How much simpler life would be if it were just a game, like tennis.

Anyone for golf? Off we go for a quick eighteen holes and then throw the clubs into a cupboard and forget them until the mood returns. It is all too rare for golf to hold its victims so lightly. For convenience we call it a game. It is supposed to be a game. But in reality, whatever else it may be, golf is not a game. The word "game" means a leisure activity performed for enjoyment in competition against an

HOLDING CLUB—CORRECT POSITION.

FIRST LESSONS IN GOLF.

BY CASPAR W. WHITNEY.

PROBABLY there is no game, unless it be court-tennis, that requires so complete a mastery of first principles and such faithful practice in its rudimentary strokes as golf. The elementary instruction of every game is of course most important, and its thorough adaptation by the pupil necessary

FRONT VIEW—BEGINNING OF THREE-QUARTER SWING.

FRONT VIEW—ENDING OF THREE-QUARTER SWING.

to the development of highest skill. In golf, however, as well as in tennis, one may never acquire consistent form if he has not started off properly. He may ride a bicycle, play lawn-tennis, baseball, box, and even fence in a duffer sort of way, yet make a fair showing and have good sport, but he cannot play golf until he has mastered the very first strokes. Herein lies the fascination of the game, which, while appearing so simple to the on-looker, becomes most difficult when he takes a club and makes his first attempt at driving off the tee.

It is not that there are so many intricate rules in golf, but the few must be mastered thoroughly, and it is well for the beginner to remember that one of England's champions declares it takes six months, playing three times a week, before one may be said to have acquired consistent form.

First of all let me say that no single chapter can give all the instruction necessary to cover the different strokes and situations arising in golf. This paper is intended solely for beginners, to whom I shall hope to give a few suggestions founded on sorrowful experience and a careful study of the game in its home. The illustrations of positions are from instantaneous photographs of Willie Dunn, son of the famous Willie Dunn deceased, contemporary of "old" Tom Morris, with whom he had many a golfing battle over Scotland's links. Dunn's form is said—by those who know—to be the very best, and we commend a study of the photographs to American golfers.

CHOOSING CLUBS.—The golfer of to-day uses more iron clubs than formerly, probably because of the substitution of gutta-percha for feather-stuffed leather balls, but more largely on account of the ingenuity of manufacturers, that has provided different-shaped heads for different "lies" of the ball. Then, too, experience has taught that certain situations require heavier and stiffer clubs for the best work. Really good clubs are hard to get, and the beginner will do well to trust their purchase to some one who is experienced. They must not be too heavy, else they overbalance the player, but the shafts should be stiffish and of hickory, which is commonly used and the best. Orange wood and ash have been employed, but neither is so good as hickory. The heads of the wooden clubs should be of beech; other woods are harder, but it is not well to have it so, as the driving quality is lessened thereby. Remember, the more the face is laid back on all your clubs, the higher they will loft the ball. Straight-faced drivers and brassies drive farther and tend to more accurate play. Do not use extreme clubs of any kind; choose the one that experience has taught is the best for the play, and if you do your part properly the club will do the rest. There is somewhat of a fad among inexperienced players to buy, for large sums, clubs that professionals have used; but it is a futile extravagance; you may get just as good ones if you use judgment in their selection. The number of different clubs put on the market of late years is considerable, and new patents are constantly being taken out, but, as a matter of fact, seven are all any one needs, viz., driver, brassy, cleek, iron, lofter, mashie, putter.

FRONT VIEW—BEGINNING OF HIGH-LOFTING STROKE.

FRONT VIEW—FINISH OF HIGH-LOFTING STROKE.

Willie Dunn uses only six—driver, brassy, cleek, iron, lofter, niblick—and putts off the cleek. On the other side, as a rule, first-class golfers use seven — driver, brassy, cleek, iron, lofter, mashie, and wooden putter; they use the last for ten-yard putts or over, and under that distance the cleek.

Driver.—Wooden club used off the tee, and thereafter whenever the lie is good enough. There are two kinds—straight-faced and bulgers; the latter, from the oval conformation of the head, are more difficult to handle, but, if you hit true, are better for straight driving. Beginners had best use straight-faced ones until they are absolutely certain of hitting where they aim. The bulger is only for the skilled player. Pick out a stiffish club, and execute the waggle to see how it feels in the hands—it should have a pronounced pliability down towards the head.

Brassy.—Wooden club, soled with iron, to be used where the lie of ball is not good enough for driver or the distance is less than full drive. It should be shorter and stiffer of shaft, and more laid back in face to raise the ball.

Cleek.—Iron club used for worse lie than brassy and shorter distance. Beginners are apt to use it for all driving, which is a mistake. If you cannot handle the regular driver (also a mistaken basis to start from, because you should persevere until you can manage it), have one made with shorter and stiffer handle. It is bad to begin your driving off iron. The cleek should be shorter than brassy,

FRONT VIEW—BEGINNING OF FULL SWING FOR DRIVING—CORRECT POSITION.

BACK VIEW—BEGINNING OF FULL SWING FOR DRIVING—INCORRECT POSITION.

and shaft stiffer. Choose thick heads, always remembering what is gained in loft is lost in distance. The blade is narrower than that of the lofter or iron; in fact, it has the straightest face next to putter.

Iron.—Shorter and stiffer shaft, and face more laid back than cleek. Is used for shorter distances than that club, and for playing out of long grass or what is called a bad lie. There are three kinds—driving, lofting, and heavy. Choose a medium one, with face not too straight nor too much laid back.

Mashie.—Compromise between iron and niblick, and has come to be used very generally now in place of the latter. Shorter and stiffer than iron, face laid farther back. Used for shorter strokes and for getting out of bunker, rut in road, long grass, or very bad lie. Beginners had better stick to iron, as the face of mashie, and especially of niblick, is so small as to require accuracy in hitting, though they pitch the ball deader.

Lofter.—Face most laid back of all the clubs. Used by experienced players with great skill in pitching ball dead on approach shot. Used largely for getting out of sand and over hazards; generally where it is desired to raise the ball in its flight.

Putter.—There has always been considerable controversy over the relative merits of the iron and wooden putter, and some of the old Scotch school have never become reconciled to the more modern metal. It is very generally conceded, however, by first-class players that wooden is best for long putts, and iron for short ones. The latter is a trifle laid back, and puts a drag on the ball, making it run off closer to the ground. When you become a veteran you can use metal for short putts, and add a wooden one to your clubs for long ones.

HOLDING CLUB.—Do not grip the club tightly, nor yet loosely; the dividing line is narrow but distinct. You should feel the shaft with fingers and palm more firmly with left than right hand. Have the hands close together, the right in front of left; remember that every inch separating them means yards off the flight of ball. A loose grip argues uncertain driving; too tight with right hand, a tendency to slice the ball. Mr. Hutchinson and Willie Dunn advise both thumbs over the club, the left a trifle more so than right.

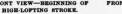

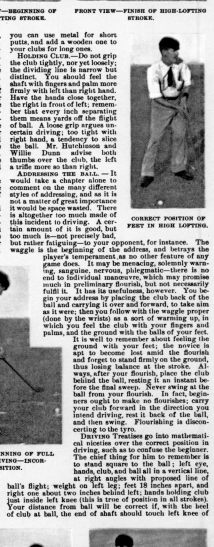

CORRECT POSITION OF FEET IN HIGH LOFTING.

ADDRESSING THE BALL.—It would take a chapter alone to comment on the many different styles of addressing, and as it is not a matter of great importance it would be space wasted. There is altogether too much made of this incident to driving. A certain amount of it is good, but too much is—not precisely bad, but rather fatiguing—to your opponent, for instance. The waggle is the beginning of the address, and betrays the player's temperament as no other feature of any game does. It may be menacing, solemnly warning, sanguine, nervous, phlegmatic—there is no end to individual manœuvre, which may promise much in preliminary flourish, but not necessarily fulfil it. It has its usefulness, however. You begin your address by placing the club back of the ball and carrying it over and forward, to take aim as it were; then you follow with the waggle proper (done by the wrists) as a sort of warming up, in which you feel the club with your fingers and palms, and the ground with the balls of your feet.

It is well to remember about feeling the ground with your feet; the novice is apt to become lost amid the flourish and forget to stand firmly on the ground, thus losing balance at the stroke. Always, after your flourish, place the club behind the ball, resting it an instant before the final sweep. Never swing at the ball from your flourish. In fact, beginners ought to make no flourishes; carry your club forward in the direction you intend driving, rest it back of the ball, and then swing. Flourishing is disconcerting to the tyro.

DRIVING Treatises go into mathematical niceties over the correct position in driving, such as to confuse the beginner. The chief thing for him to remember is to stand square to the ball; left eye, hands, club, and ball all in a vertical line, at right angles with proposed line of ball's flight; weight on left leg; feet 18 inches apart, and right one about two inches behind left; hands holding club just inside left knee (this is true of position in all strokes). Your distance from ball will be correct if, with the heel of club at ball, the end of shaft should touch left knee of

FRONT VIEW—PUTTING. CORRECT POSITION.

FRONT VIEW—PUTTING. INCORRECT POSITION.

LOFTING A STIMIE.

THE WAGGLE.

FRONT VIEW—GETTING OUT OF
A BUNKER.

BACK VIEW—BEGINNING OF FULL SWING
FOR DRIVING—CORRECT POSITION.

FRONT VIEW—BEGINNING OF FULL
SWING FOR DRIVING—INCOR-
RECT POSITION.

playes as he stands upright. Incidentally, remember, as distance for stroke decreases, have the ball nearer right toe.

The closer the feet the freer the swing, but if too close, the driving is apt to be weakened and inaccurate; with feet far apart, the player becomes stiffened, shortening the drive, though gaining great power. In the swing, bear in mind that as your club goes up so it will come down; slow up swing, relatively speaking, is a *sine qua non* of fine driving. Regard the left arm as part of the club, and keep it taut. The greatest amount of practice is necessary to allow arms to swing well away, and yet bring them down and in, for the club must be travelling in the intended flight of ball when brought down. Mr. Horace Hutchinson, whose Badminton volume is far and away the most complete, instructive, and interesting of anything published on the game, explains this point clearly thus: Take a spot on the ground, and then draw away your club. You will find the only way to extend the proposed line of flight, *backward*, is to straighten out the arms well; if you bend them, you find the head of club leaving the line. In the up swing, left arm should rest comfortably across chest, slightly bent at elbow; do not pause at top of swing; increase speed as you bring club downward, and get in your power when about 18 inches from the ball.

At the moment of hitting the ball you must be in precisely the same position as at the time of addressing it. This is the difficulty of golf, and can only be acquired by patient, persistent practice. There is no short-cut to golfing success. Remember to *sweep* away the ball, a sort of scythe motion; the beginner is likely to think only of hitting it; never jerk your club except in bunker or similar hazard. Do not tighten up when you strike the ball, nor try to knock it out of sight. Be easy, follow the ball with your club, and keep your feet on the ground. Hit fairly, clearly, firmly, not wildly.

Do not bother about too much detail at first. A beginner is likely to ask and be given no end of confusing and oftentimes worthless advice. He should seek competent counsel, and should then follow it, bearing in mind he must practise for weeks and months before he will have any form. He is apt to do better the first few times he plays, when he has no thought of style, and is intent only on whacking the ball, than a little later. Golf is learned by imitation largely, and it is likewise, more than any other game, full of mimics. It is not good to become one of the latter, because mannerisms are not of the slightest value, and are to be avoided. Watch good form; try to attain a free style, and practise with that end constantly in view. It is not possible, of course, for all men to have the same style. A very heavy man cannot expect to get the swing and freedom of a more athletically built one. Each player has a style that, starting (or at least it should start) from the one basis, is the reflection of the age at which he began, and of himself physically and mentally.

There is a great deal of buncombe about the waggle and style, the importance of both being greatly exaggerated. What the beginner need concern himself about is to get accuracy; keep the club travelling in the direction of the ball after the strike, and follow with the body; get the shoulders into the sweep, the entire body, in fact; bear weight on left leg at the address, transferring it to right on up swing, and again to the left as the ball is swept away. Let the lifting of knee and left heel on up swing be incidental to the swing, *i.e.*, you must not set out to do it—it will come in season. Stand steady, feeling the ground with your feet, keep direction of swing right, and the eye *always* on the ball. Above all, keep your mind on the business of the moment; think of what you are trying to do; beginners are inclined to fancy golf so simple as to require no special mental application. Never play weakly; remember the length of swing and not strength of sweep regulates carry of the ball. Use weaker clubs instead of making weaker effort. A full shot is the full swing; three-quarter shot, shoulders do not turn, work being done by arms, legs, and hips; half shot, use arms from elbow-joints only; quarter shot is chiefly made by wrists.

Concentrate your efforts on learning to get the swing (no matter whether you hit the ball or not at first, hitting is of small importance compared with get-

ting the swing properly), to drive straight; play out of a bad lie and loft out of a hole. When you can do these things in some degree of form you may call yourself a golfer. It is not enough to learn to drive. You must drive straight, that is important, else you get off the course, and lose considerably. This is where the value of accuracy makes itself apparent. Remember the injunction not to use the cleek for driving, and remember also, if you do, that the "divots" (sods) you cut out should be replaced at once. Practise with the driver until you master it—in fact, make it a point to take that club which puzzles you and work with it until you control it.

Most golf play is made up of driving, iron play, and putting, and of these driving is the most pleasing. Iron clubs are much the best for approaching the putting green, and you should endeavor always to lay your ball dead.

An approach shot is one within sixty yards of the green, and it is difficult play. Only your instructor can give you the practical instruction that is needed here. But bear in mind that in all iron shots you play off your right foot—*i. e.*, right foot in advance (whereas in driving left foot is in advance), weight on left leg—ball distant the length of

BACK VIEW—ENDING OF FULL
SWING AFTER DRIVE—COR-
RECT POSITION.

FRONT VIEW—ENDING OF FULL
SWING AFTER DRIVE—INCOR-
RECT POSITION.

FRONT VIEW OF FEET
FOR DRIVING—CORRECT
POSITION.

BEGINNING OF HALF IRON SHOT.
CORRECT POSITION.

ENDING OF HALF IRON SHOT.
CORRECT POSITION.

FRONT VIEW OF FEET
FOR DRIVING—INCOR-
RECT POSITION.

club to left knee, as in driving, and on a line that would run about midway between feet.

Putting is the least interesting and very important, though

many ignore, or rather slight it, because of the difficulty, which is greater than in driving. Many a game has been won on the green. Practise long and carefully, but be sure you have a well-balanced club. Hit smoothly without jerk. Putt with the wrists. Let the club work from them, in fact, as a pendulum. Assume a position from which you can best send the putter straight as it meets the ball. Stand open, half facing hole, weight slightly on left leg, right foot in advance, ball equal distance between feet. In short putts of three or four yards and less, rest right elbow on thigh; be sure of the *exact* spot on putter that will hit the ball; hold club with both hands equally, and always "be up"—*i. e.*, putt strong enough to reach the hole. It is better to pass it than not strong enough to reach it.

The pleasure of golf depends very considerably on the quality of ground. Your links must not be too easy, nor yet too difficult, and the carries (distances from tee over bunker) should not be too long, so that the medium driver may have a chance. There should be plenty of hazards, so arranged that every hole is guarded. In fact, for good golf a difficulty should be put in the way of every shot. Putting greens (and our American ones, generally speaking, are very poor) should be about thirty yards in diameter, and the hole ought to be moved when worn. Greens should be absolutely clear of obstruction and as smooth as possible. I mention this because so many that are planning homemade links seem to think the green should have its share of trials. There is tribulation enough on the green without increasing it by hazards. In building bunkers throw up the ground on the farther side, so the excavation becomes part of the hazard; the bunker should slant from the player (not straight-faced), and the bank be wide.

I follow with a few definitions in reply to the many letters received on the subject. *Links* is the course of holes—18 being the regulation, but 12 is the largest number on any links in America, though Shinnecock intends lengthening its 12 to 18. *Tee*—starting-point. *Caddie*—generally speaking, the boy that carries your clubs—on the other side, however, he is often counsellor and father-confessor. To *foozle* or *duff* a shot means to bungle it. *Topping*—not hitting well behind the ball. *Slicing*—bringing club down with a cut instead of squarely. *Heeling*—hitting ball with heel of club. *Toeing*—hitting with toe. *Fore* is called at the time of driving to warn players in front of you.

Two holes up means you are leading the opponent by two holes. *Dormie*—when you are leading your opponent by as many holes as there are left to play, so that were he to win all remaining, he could only tie you; for instance, if you were two-up and two to play.

Stimie is the situation where your opponent's ball is between yours and the hole, and more than 6 inches separating the two balls. You are obliged to loft over it; if the balls were within 6 inches of each other you could remove opponent's ball while you played.

He whose ball is behind always plays first.

Those on putting green are entitled to hole out before following ones play up to it.

Players in front are each entitled to second shot before following players tee off.

Do not talk while player is making his shot. Keep away 5 to 6 yards, and stand at side—never behind.

Never go on green while others are playing there. A four

BACK VIEW—ENDING OF FULL SWING
AFTER DRIVE—INCORRECT POSITION.

FRONT VIEW—ENDING OF FULL SWING
AFTER DRIVE—CORRECT POSITION.

ADDRESSING BALL FOR
DRIVE—CORRECT POSITION.

opponent. When Jones plays Smith at tennis this definition usually applies. They play against each other, enjoy the recreation, and eventually one of them wins.

But what happens when Jones and Smith go to golf? Jones plays against Jones, while simultaneously Smith does battle with Smith. Each man is involved in a struggle with himself, trying to discipline his muscles and control the seething anarchy in his mind. In golf, as Bobby Jones has shown us, every man is his own opponent and it hardly matters what his human adversary is doing. Nobody influences what happens to your ball except yourself. There are no high-kicking serves or cunning drop volleys to counter. The ball sits there quite still and, it seems at times, insolently mocks you. If you don't hit it properly it is no one's fault but your own. There are no excuses in golf, although man exercises his ingenuity to find them.

No matter how we may tell each other that we had a stinking bad lie or, as with the P. G. Wodehouse character, we were put off by the uproar of the butterflies in the next meadow, we know deep down that we fluffed it. Golfers are almost pathological

about cursing their luck. What they are really doing, of course, is trying to salvage the last shreds of their self-esteem. When all else fails—when the lie is palpably good and even the butterflies hold their racket for the moment—the golfer who misses the shot is forced to the ultimate desperation of blaming his failure on supernatural forces. Bad luck. Some people may even convince themselves for the moment that they are indeed the victims of malicious forces. But deep inside the golfer the dreadful truth, too shaming to admit even to oneself, registers on the subconscious.

"Whom do you think you are kidding?" asks Subconscious. "Mea culpa. It wasn't bad luck, but bad me. Idiot me. Stupid, uncoordinated me. How is it possible that a genuine half-wit, like that young assistant pro, can score almost as low as his I.Q., while an intelligent, strong, and virile fellow like me can't break a hundred, even playing Mulligans?" Conscious self says, "It will be better next time. I can do it." Subconscious self knows that it will be as bad as ever, for subconscious self is the saboteur who causes those shanks and feeble, half-topped drives.

17

Early fanaticism: in print—with Harper's *1894 instruction (preceding pages); in fun—Scotland's "Golf-Stream" (opposite above); in extremis—drawing by A. B. Frost (bottom); and in frustration—with a cruel lie (above).*

It is, then, in the murky regions of the psyche that the competitive element of golf is found. This is why golf is the loneliest game and why, once the conflict is joined, it grips with obsessional power. It may even explain the bittersweet story of the man who was bitten by the golfing bug early in life but could never really get the hang of the game. For forty years he played three times a week at his club without any distinction at all. Fate smiles occasionally on all of us and it is true that on several occasions this golfer played the first seventeen holes in quite respectable figures. Once, in his middle seventies on a calm summer evening, he needed a 4 at the last to equal par. This 18th was not long, only 380 yards, but it was an old-fashioned blind hole and reputedly a card wrecker. The drive was over the brow of a hill, and beyond this crest the fairway sloped sharply down to a pond on the left. If you drove too far right you found thick bushes. It was a tricky drive to be sure, absurdly tight, and by modern standards unfair. However, the club members took a perverse pride in their killer hole and nothing would persuade them to modify its terrors. Most people soon learned to play it as a par-5, popping a gentle iron to the top of the hill on the second shot, and then gingerly nudging another iron to a position from which a chip to the green might leave a single putt for the par.

This particular golfer would have no truck with such cowardly tactics. "Better to die like a man," he would announce, pulling the headcover off his driver, "than live like a chicken. It is only a drive and a pitch." His bravado was skin deep. Inwardly quaking, he automatically tightened his grip on the club, failed to complete his backswing in the belief that he was executing a compact, controlled stroke, and without fail, three times a week for forty years, he either flat-hooked into the pond or hit a high slice into the bushes. It is a matter of simple mathematics to calculate that he had played the hole something like six thousand times. He had never scored better than a 5.

The camera as Impressionist conveys whirling, blurring, imprecise mind of the golfer as he attacks the enemy.

Now he faced that drive again, and not for a minute did he consider any other club than his driver. Anyway, at the age of seventy-five, he needed all the length he could get, especially as it had been raining for most of the week and there would not be much run on the ball. He carefully selected a choice spot to tee his ball and took his stance. As he strained every muscle in that premature lunge his right foot slipped slightly on the muddy tee. It was only a tiny skid, less than one inch, but vital. The effect was to throw the arc of his clubhead into a slightly different plane and to delay its impact momentarily. The differences were infinitesimal, but when you consider that the clubface is in contact with the ball for only half of a thousandth of a second, you can appreciate that the difference between a good shot and a bad one is a matter of fine adjustment.

The difference in this case was dramatic. The clubhead caught the ball exactly right, flush on the button, and square. The meaty "crack" of impact and that indescribable, sensuous tremor of the club told him that he had hit such a drive as he had never hit before. He held his follow-through position like a statue and perhaps, after forty years, we can forgive him this little vanity. No bullet from a rifle ever flew straighter nor, it seemed, faster as it pierced the air on a line directly above the center of the fairway. Nothing could prevent it from carrying clear to that flat area of fairway from which he would have a routine pitch for a simple 4, possibly a birdie. Nothing could prevent it? The ball hit a marker post planted on the brow of the hill. The impact was almost as loud as the blow from the club. The ball rebounded straight back with hardly diminished speed. It pitched, bounced twice, rolled onto the tee and came gently to rest against the leg of the prostrate (and dead) golfer. The expression on his face was quizzical. "Why?" he seemed to be asking. "Why?" They buried the ball with him.

That golfer, and we all know him, tells us

Human frailties—and the golfer certainly has his share—are source of most of the game's comedy. Here cartoons of Clare Briggs from the twenties.

something about the game. It can be a lifelong crusade, and if such golfers do not always end in a figurative snowdrift clasping a banner with a strange device, at least Longfellow would understand the unswerving sense of purpose which directs their lives.

There are many other types of the genus golfer, not least the remarkable man who loves to hate the game. Of this variety there can be few more extreme examples than the business executive who, since happily he is still among us, must be identified only by his initials, R. G. He was a man of prodigious energy. The air positively tingled with static when R. G. was switched on, which was most of the time. He had little formal education, but a good mind and a flair for getting straight to the essentials of the most complicated problem. As a result of these gifts, his career (in magazine publishing) had been spectacular. Like most people with a quick brain, he was impatient with those who were slower to grasp an idea and he made little attempt to control his feelings.

Whether a quick temper is the result of high blood pressure, or the other way round, is a matter for doctors to argue. At all events, by the age of fifty-two R. G. had undergone two medical crises serious enough for him to be ordered to give up his fifty-a-day addiction to cigarettes and all forms of alcohol.

NOW JUST-A-MOMENT-PLEASE! BEFORE YOU DISAPPEAR FOR THE SUMMER--- GIVE US A RING ONCE IN A WHILE- IT ONLY COSTS A NICKEL TO TELEPHONE IF YOU ARE GOING TO BE LATE FOR DINNER--- REMEMBER YOU HAVE A WIFE AND FAMILY TO SUPPORT SO GIVE A LITTLE ATTENTION TO BUSINESS--- AND INCIDENTALLY LEAVE US A LITTLE CASH BEFORE YOU GO- WE MAY NEED FOOD AND CLOTHING BEFORE YOU RETURN

Within another year the pace again caught up with him. This time the cardiac specialist issued an ultimatum: If R. G. continued to push himself at this pace it would be tantamount to suicide. It wasn't just a risk but a certainty. Retirement was his only chance. "Get out of the rat race and take it easy. You've made your packet. Relax and enjoy it."

R. G., who was still under light sedation, agreed. Encouraged by his success, the specialist, who rather fancied himself a psychiatrist, tossed out a suggestion: "Ever tried golf?" His reasoning was that a man who had led such an active life would certainly be unable to switch to a regime of tending his roses. He would need an interest, and what better release for tension could be found than the gentle physical activity of golf? A healthy open-air pursuit would safely absorb those restless energies. "Golf?" said R. G. "Never had time for that sort of nonsense." "I'll send you a book about it," said the specialist, "and when you're up and about, you might like to come out to my club. We've got quite a decent bunch of members and you can see how you like the idea of the game."

Next day a package arrived at R. G.'s bedside. It was a copy of Ben Hogan's *Modern Fundamentals of Golf* and the gardener who retrieved it from the hospital grounds said later that it had flown from

R. G.'s window "as if fired from a howitzer."

The specialist might have taken warning from this incident. R. G.'s fury apparently had been aroused by the title. If golf was a sixteenth-century game, then its fundamentals could not be called modern, he said. And if, on the other hand, Hogan had meant the basic principles of a new golfing method he should have called his book *The Fundamentals of Modern Golf*. "That man's a sloppy thinker," said R. G.

The specialist was not deterred. Golf, he remained convinced, would be excellent therapy for his patient. Wisely, he made no attempt to defend Hogan. Ignoring the calumny on the most precise mind in golf, he went ahead and booked a lesson for R. G. with the club professional, a quiet lowland Scot with an uncanny ability to measure a golfer's potential at a glance. R. G. was an easy diagnosis. Handmade shoes meant money and the general air of the man was manic-obsessive. With the right encouragement he would be good for a new set of clubs every year, possibly two sets. "You've got the look of a golfer about you," he told R. G. as they walked to the teaching area. "Good hands and power in those legs." R. G. had a certain respect for technical experts, up to a point, and allowed himself to absorb two pieces of advice: that acquiring a correct grip was worth perseverance, even though it might feel unnatural at the beginning; and that unless you set yourself up properly it was impossible to hit the ball consistently.

That was enough instruction for R. G. "Let me hit one," he commanded. The pro put down a ball and R. G. carefully took his stance. What happened next was a parody of golf, a flashing, whirling, violent convulsion. The components of the swing—slow takeaway, transfer of weight to right foot, cocking of the wrists, return shift of weight, and smooth sweep of the clubhead through the ball—were compressed into a frenzied blur. The outcome, however, was all too clear. The ball, almost severed into two hemispheres,

Evidence that golf should and can
be a visual experience with
examples from Bermuda's Mid-Ocean and (above)
Sugarbush Country Club, Vermont.

scuttled about twenty yards. "Good God!" said R. G. "Give me another."

The pro put down a second ball and the process was repeated in exact manner, except that this time R. G.'s exclamation was uttered with a tone of less surprise and more acerbity. "Another."

The third attempt was identical. "Ball!"

The pro teed up another sacrificial victim. This lesson was beginning to work out expensively in murdered balls. "If you'd just . . ." "Shut up!" shouted R. G., decapitating another ball, "and give me another blasted pill."

There are, reflected the pro, two kinds of pupils: those who are willing and able to learn the game properly and those who are beyond redemption. R. G. was clearly of the second category. With these unteachables, all you could do was to make minor remedial adjustments to the contortions they called a swing in order that they could make some sort of contact. This time he positioned the ball opposite R. G.'s left heel. If that slashing attack returned the club to the same place there was just a chance. He had to do something. Judging by the vermilion flush rising from this character's collar, there was danger of losing a valuable customer for good.

This time, R. G.'s dervish onslaught ended with a crisp metallic click which golfers recognize as the sweetest note in the harmonic scale. The ball, first boring, then soaring, then seeming to hang in the sky, fell far down the fairway. "Got it," said R. G. "Didn't I say you were a natural?" said the pro.

This was the revelatory flash of magic every golfer experiences once, the moment when the virus gets into the bloodstream. In that second was born the most evil-tempered golfer in the history of the game. R. G. did have a certain facility for golf, and there are those who believe that if his temperament had been less volatile he could have been very good, indeed. However, the one golfing axiom which brooks no ex-

ceptions is that controlled golf and an uncontrolled temper can never coexist. Even when things were going well, R. G. was cantankerous and complained at every step. He played golf like a man drawing his own teeth.

In the long history of the game there has never been a flawless round. Bobby Jones perhaps came nearest to it; his 66 in qualifying for the 1926 British Open, at Sunningdale, near London, is often recalled as the closest approach to perfection, but even that exhibition of accuracy contained blemishes, at least by R. G.'s hair-trigger standards. Jones did not one-putt every green, for instance. For R. G., of course, a miss from 30 feet was enough to light the fuse. He fought it, but you could see that he had not fully regained his composure by the time he teed up at the next hole. That meant a stray drive and a fearsome oath, often compounded by a smashing of the club into the turf, or, as on one memorable occasion, the violent destruction of a tee box. Usually he managed to hold himself in until, still seething, he hit his second shot. That's when he popped his cork. His club-throwing technique was highly developed and he achieved huge distances. Once he threw his five-iron so far into the shrubbery that he could not find it. As always, once the safety valve had been opened, he was immediately contrite. "That's my favorite club," he moaned. "What am I going to do?" Any opponents who tried the classic reply, "Go back and throw another," were rewarded with a look of black hatred.

R. G. was good at hating. He found reason for dissatisfaction with his best shots, and never once in five years had he been known to show signs of pleasure or even satisfaction on the course. It couldn't go on. What with the complaining and explosions of fury the inevitable day came when, having put two balls and his four-wood out of bounds in quick succession, he had another seizure. They carried him in and made him comfortable on a bench in the locker room while the secretary telephoned the heart specialist. "This won't

Another cartoonist who loved golf was New York Herald-Tribune's *H. T. Webster, whose favorite butt was Caspar Milquetoast, the timid soul.*

Head down in concentration
(at Wee Burn in Connecticut) and head
up in glorious fulfillment (at
Puerto Rico's spectacular El Conquistador).

do," the doctor told R. G., after giving him an injection. "I'm sorry, old chap, I'm afraid you'll just have to give up golf." "What!" shouted R. G., fighting the sedative. "You made me stop smoking and you made me give up drink. Now golf. Dammit, it's the only pleasure I've got left."

So far, then, we have seen golf as a form of madness and an instrument of torture. Surely there is more to it than that. Cannot it also be good clean fun and healthy exercise, beneficial to the body and at the same time a civilizing influence on the character? Well, maybe. But when it comes to the *mens sana in corpore sano* syndrome, the muddled oafs and flanneled fools of the other popular games have the advantage.

Golf is not energetic enough for a muscular tonic. You have only to watch someone like Julius Boros playing golf to realize that for sweating off surplus poundage you would be better off with a furious game of dominoes. The proliferation of motorized buggies to transport the golfer between shots and carry the ice bucket, glasses, and martinis is to be deplored if only because they deny the golfer the conscience-saving excuse that golf is good for him. There is enough guilt on the course as it is, without losing the righteous glow which comes with physical exhaustion.

Golf takes many forms. In Ireland it can be miniaturized, played with only a wedge and putter, and with no hole longer than 75 yards. This pitch-and-putt version has its own separate administration and championships, and there are highly skilled players who have never played "the long game" in their lives.

In Japan it can be akin to archery, played

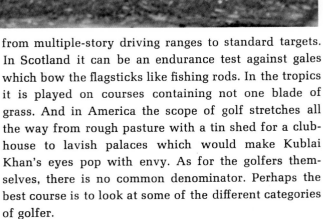

from multiple-story driving ranges to standard targets. In Scotland it can be an endurance test against gales which bow the flagsticks like fishing rods. In the tropics it is played on courses containing not one blade of grass. And in America the scope of golf stretches all the way from rough pasture with a tin shed for a clubhouse to lavish palaces which would make Kublai Khan's eyes pop with envy. As for the golfers themselves, there is no common denominator. Perhaps the best course is to look at some of the different categories of golfer.

One of the commoner types is the man with a virility complex, who sees the game as a trial of strength. He is a slugger and revels in outhitting rather than outscoring an opponent. For him the vital question is not "How many shots did you take?" but

"What club did you use?" On a short hole he will risk a double hernia getting up with a seven-iron and it does not matter if he lands in a bunker and takes three more to get down. His victory is in being pin high. You may be short with a five-iron, play a delicate run-up, and sink the putt for your par, but as far as he is concerned he has won a moral victory. There is no point in trying to deflate him by making remarks to the effect that it's not "How?" but "How many?" which counts in golf, because in his case it is not true. The only way is by beating him on his own terms, as in the following story in which only the names are fictitious.

In the annual knockout competition of a golfing society, the finalists who emerged were a bull-like creature we shall call King, a considerable player when things were going his way, and Peabody, a steady

Rain or shine, the putting ritual transcends meteorology—at New York's Leewood Golf Club and (right) under Minnesota's big skies at Bemidji.

player and a man of modest skills whose main strength was determination and a certain low cunning.

Peabody realized that his only chance was to attack King's muscular vanity, and to this end he had his pro make up a driver forty-six inches long, or four inches longer than normal. With this club Peabody practiced in secret for a week. The final was played on a course which began with a long-short hole, about 190 yards, and Peabody won the toss. His four-wood found the edge of the green and King was just through the back with a four-iron. They halved in threes and at the 420-yard 2nd Peabody played a three-wood and a four-wood, while King got up with a driver and a seven-iron. Another half, and King was beginning to swell up with self-satisfaction. In his terms he was slaughtering Peabody and the outcome was only a matter of time.

The 3rd hole was a monster, well over 500 yards, and the fairway was generously wide. Peabody teed up his ball, drew out his 46-inch driver, and removed its headcover prominently marked "2." It was the slowest swing you ever saw, as it must be with a

club like that. To King it looked like a lazy, halfhearted effort—which was exactly what Peabody intended him to think. "Just a gentle little brassie should do me," said Peabody as he watched the ball howl off down the fairway. King could hardly believe his eyes. He stepped grimly onto the tee with his driver and wound himself up for what was to be the biggest drive of his life. Measured strictly in terms of applied energy it might have been. But as we all know, distance is achieved not by hitting the ball harder, but better. And the violence of King's swing threw the clubhead off line. The ball zoomed away in a high slice, landing in the rough a 100 yards short of Peabody's ball. For all practical purposes the match ended there.

Peabody said nothing. Words were unnecessary, although many a lesser man would have been tempted to crow over his victim. He simply smiled a private smile, such as Delilah, scissors in hand, must have smiled after shearing Samson's locks.

He did not use the secret weapon again. For one thing, there was no other hole on the course

*Satisfying shot to the green
(at Wee Burn) and frustrating search
for the ball (at Spyglass in
California) are all part of the game.*

with a fairway wide enough to give him the necessary confidence. Anyway, it was superfluous. King, trying to hit harder and harder and harder, was all over the place. His timing had gone and his power was dissipated in a succession of half-tops and fluffs. By the end of the match Peabody was outhitting him, club for club, without any effort. It was a full month before King got his game going again.

Another subspecies known to country-club anthropologists is the Stylist. He can be recognized before he hits a shot. On the first tee you see him meticulously plaiting his fingers around the club. He coils to the top of his backswing and holds the position; his head turns to admire the straight line of left forearm and wrist and to check the angle of the clubface. This ritual is followed by a performance like a slide show of the various positions of the swing. Click! He slides his hips to the left. Click! He brings his hands to waist level with the right elbow tucked unnaturally close to his navel. Click! He makes an imaginary pass through an imaginary ball. Click! He stretches up to a classic follow-through position.

This routine may be followed half a dozen times before he is reassured that he has mastered every point in the latest magazine instructional article. The shot, when he eventually plays it, shows little resemblance to the slow-motion pantomime on the tee and the result seldom bears out the promise of the article or book which he has been reading ("Let Billy Casper show you how to knock ten strokes off your handicap"). And every time the Stylist hits a bad shot he remains rooted to the spot, performing a dumb show of the stroke he should have played.

It is not within the scope of this book (nor within the competence of the author, for that matter) to offer advice on how to play golf. But it is perhaps in order to suggest a method of clipping the Stylist, since the noble techniques of winning at golf go far beyond hitting the ball correctly.

The thing to do with a Stylist is to watch him closely for a few holes and deduce whom he is trying to copy. Stylists usually overdo it and will go as far as to ape the mannerisms of their hero. Thus, a Snead fantasy frequently includes the adoption of a straw hat. Now, having determined that your opponent believes himself to be a replica of Slamming Sam, you casually drop what the golfing gamesman calls a contra-suggestion. You might, for instance, say, "I can't help feeling that Doug Sanders has a point when he says that there is less room for error with a short backswing. I mean, it sounds logical."

That is a glaringly blatant specimen of contrasuggestion and with practice a skilled practitioner can refine the process to extremes of subtlety. One Stylist was completely thrown by a fractional raising of his opponent's eyebrow at a vital stage in the match. The tiniest grain of sand can grow into a fat pearl of doubt and confusion.

A rarer specimen, though a no less odious creature for that, is the Scorer. He cares nothing for style and takes no satisfaction in a well-struck shot. He normally can be identified by his hickory-shafted putter bound in several places with tape, and he usually is of Scottish descent. Often enough his clubs are a mongrel collection picked up over the years from the bargain barrel. Beware this man, for he is fireproof. He is immune to all forms of verbal gamesmanship and is in no way upset by being outdriven. You, with your natural flair for the game, boom your drives past him and produce a dazzling display of virtuoso shots. He doesn't even notice, let alone care. Where your shots come off the clubface with a report like a revolver shot, his go "plop." He has never hit the green of a par-5 hole with two shots in his life and, what is more, he has never tried. You annihilate him. And then you add up the scores at the end of the round and find he has beaten you by five shots. That should be lesson enough. Steer clear of him, for if you play with him often enough you are doomed to madness and despair.

These three basic categories of golfer, with numerous subspecies and hybrids, are, however, genuine golfers. The game is also peopled by those who do not so much play golf as play at golf.

There are social golfers for whom membership in an exclusive country club is a prop to an inferiority complex, or simply proof of their standing in the community. And there is a substantial category to whom golf is a business asset. There was a time when a bleached left hand was a badge of the professional; now it is just as likely to signify an insurance salesman, hustlers both.

Among these diverse types there is possibly one common characteristic, a universal capacity for self-deception. For some obscure reason, golfers of all standards, from the worst hacker to the mightiest professional, employ a defense mechanism which consists, to put it bluntly, of lying about their putting.

Is "lie" too strong a word? Let us examine a typical witness. A 2-handicap player goes round in 80 and explains to anyone he can trap in a corner of the locker room, "I couldn't buy a putt." In such circumstances most of us mutter some formal expression of condolence such as "rotten luck," and duck for safety. (It is one of the natural laws of golf that there is no more boring experience in life than listening to reports of other people's rounds, while, paradoxically, our own shot-by-shot accounts are spellbinding in their fascination.)

However, back to putting. If we can fight off the involuntary glazing of the eye and spontaneous twitching of the jaw muscles when our 2-handicap friend launches into his dreary recital of putting, we can crucify him on the cross of his own miserable conscience. We stand our ground, feign a look of lively interest, and say, "Trouble on the greens, eh? Tell me about it. How did it go on the first hole, for instance?" He may be taken aback by this unconventional response, but such is the vanity of golfers that he will certainly replay every shot for your benefit. Ignore all his guff about the diabolical luck when his drive kicked into the rough and the wedge slipped in his hand. Take note of the putts. Tot them up and confront him with the total: "I make that thirty-five putts altogether. You're *supposed* to take thirty-six. The truth is that you played like an idiot and now you're trying to blame your lamentable score on the greenkeeper. Know thyself. And stop this sickening mendacity; we don't care for brazen liars in this club." Now duck for safety.

There is no shame in putting badly. Miss a green with a nine-iron and you are a figure of ridicule; miss a four-footer and the world weeps with you. Nine times out of ten, the man who complains that he putted badly really means that he didn't hit the ball close enough to give himself the chance of a good putting round. To understand may be to forgive but, yes, the self-deception of the putting excuse is still a thumping great lie.

Finally, there are also a few rare characters who are not psychological cripples or charlatans or social climbers but are well-adjusted individuals who simply enjoy golf for what it is. Here we may enjoy a slightly conspiratorial liaison, because it so happens that you are just such a golfer. And, come to think of it, looking around at your circle of golfing acquaintances, you are the only one with a rational and adult attitude to the game. Isn't that so? What an extraordinary coincidence.

But all golfers, we must hope, experience at some time the combination of a glorious day, a beautiful course, the companionship of good friends, and an effective putting stroke which can make golf the second most satisfying activity known to mankind. In the end we must conclude that there are as many answers to the question "What is golf?" as there are golfers. Golf is as varied as life itself and, in the end, like life, golf is what we make it.

the explorer who sets out to find the source of golf soon discovers that his problem is not to grope his way through unmapped territories. The geography is all too familiar. He must choose among a tracery of streams, each marked, "Genuine Source of Golf." All these signs cannot be true, or can they? Perhaps they are all tributaries of equal importance. And what of the streams which bubble up out of the rocks? Are they springs, and therefore potential candidates for the honor of being called the genuine source? Or are they nothing more than extensions of the same tributary which has just gone underground for a while? The search then becomes a laborious effort to eliminate false sources.

The point of departure must be the earliest recorded mention of the word "golf." This occurs in the year 1457 in an Act of the Scottish Parliament under King James II, known as Fiery Face, which proved to be a prophetic nickname, since he was killed when a cannon he was inspecting blew up. His decree forbade the playing of golf: "the futeball and golfe be utterly cryed downe and not to be used." The reason for this harsh enactment was that Scotland was in a more or less permanent state of war against England and every able-bodied man was required to devote his spare time to archery practice for the protection of the realm. Clearly, men had been neglecting their military training for the more congenial pastimes of kicking footballs or hitting golf balls, both, incidentally, pursuits which retain the force of a national religion in Scotland to this day. So too does the ancient rivalry against England, but nowadays the traditional obsessions are neatly combined and battles against the old enemy are mainly confined to the football field.

The dereliction of duty of those early yeomen which so threatened the efficiency of the citizen army was not new. Some thirty-three years earlier a similar decree had been issued by the Scots Parliament, but in this case football only had been banned. Golf

was not mentioned, so we can assume that in 1424 the game had not yet developed to a stage where it threatened the national security. We cannot, however, assume that it was not established in some form; indeed, it is highly unlikely that in a static medieval community, and one preoccupied with war and rebellion, any game could achieve widespread popularity over a relatively short period of time. The probability is, surely, that golf in some form was played in Scotland at least from the beginning of the fifteenth century.

Professor Douglas Young, who has written a history of St. Andrews, comes out with the bald, bold statement that golf was invented in Scotland soon after the founding of the University of St. Andrews (1414). However, his evidence in support of such a positive assertion is curiously flimsy for such a meticulous historian. We can admire the sight of a scholar crawling so far out on a limb, but perhaps it would be prudent to consider whether that precarious perch will bear the weight of our skepticism.

Until irrefutable proof is brought to light we must reserve judgment as to a specific birth date. In any case, is there a specific date to be found? The majority of historians prefer the view that one of the continental ball games was introduced into Scotland, probably by soldiers returning from European wars, and that the game gradually developed its essential golfing characteristics under local Scottish conditions. One persuasive theory is that the Scots troops, who were supporting their French allies against the British invaders, came home converts to the game of *chole*. A contemporary account describes how some Scottish officers were playing the game close to a river crossing near Bauge, when they caught sight of the standards of an English party advancing for a surprise attack. The Scots troops formed up and knocked the stuffing out of the English—one of the few reverses for England since Agincourt. That would date the importation in 1421. The origin of chole can be traced back for a fur-

Preceding pages: Portrait of members of the Royal and Ancient club in front of clubhouse on Medal Day, painted about 1890. Old Tom Morris, the patriarchal pro, is teeing the captain's ball.

36

ther three hundred years at least, so here is a possible parent of truly respectable antiquity.

Once again, however, we must scrutinize the theory for probability and common sense and, alas, it does not pass the test. Chole, a game indigenous to Belgium and northern France, has a superficial resemblance to golf. Chole clubs have iron heads resembling those of golf clubs and the game is played with a ball made of wood (as all early golf balls were). But there the similarity ends.

The basic conception of chole is entirely alien to golf. In chole, having chosen a distant target such as a barn door, one team hits the ball toward the goal while the opponents, or decholeurs, try to frustrate the process by hitting the ball back into difficult places. If chole was played by Scottish soldiers in France (as seems likely), and was brought home to Scotland by them (which is possible but conjectural), it must have undergone such a fundamental transformation as to constitute a new game altogether.

Another favored candidate as the progenitor of golf is the Dutch game of *Kolven*, especially since it is played with an instrument called a *Kolf*. Language offers other seductive clues in the Dutch expression, *"Stuit mij!"* meaning "It stops me," which therefore corresponds in sound and sense with the golfer's "stymie." And then there is the warning cry of *"Vooor,"* which fits "Fore" so neatly. There are more seemingly uncanny similarities between golfing expressions and Dutch equivalents. Unfortunately, as Robert Browning, the author of *A History of Golf,* points out with crushing logic, there is a simple explanation. "Kolf" and "golf" sound the same because they have the same origin in the German word, *Kolbe,* meaning club. The words, then, exist quite independently of the games to which they are applied.

That is all very well, but it fails to explain why the word "golf" was not established in the language before the coming of the game. Surely, people would have called any type of club a golf. However, this line of inquiry is sterile. For whatever similarities there may be in the language of golf and kolven, the games themselves are poles apart. Kolven was played with a large ball on a paved court, or on ice, and has no affinity with the national game of Scotland beyond being a club-and-ball pastime. And if we are going to round up all the club-and-ball games as suspects for our paternity suit, there is no limit to the possibilities. What about the French game of *jeu de mail,* which was played in England as pall-mall? One of London's noblest streets is named after it, but it was played with mallets and so, although it may have sired croquet, we can acquit it of responsibility for golf.

What about another French game, *jeu de paume,* which was played, as its name implies, with the palm of the hand, but with a leather ball stuffed with feathers just like the later golf balls? The feather ball, however, did not come into golf until the seventeenth century and, anyway, the ancient Romans had been making balls this way centuries previously. Possibly jeu de paume was the forerunner of tennis, fives, or handball, but we must dismiss it from the golf inquiries. *Crosse,* an ancient French game, was played with a curved stick or club and that is about as much as we know about it, so crosse too must be released from the case for lack of evidence.

If we follow up every ball-and-club game, the quest will be endless. We know such games were played by the early Greeks, and that the Romans amused themselves with one called *paganica.* And such games probably go back much further than that; it is the most natural action in the world, having picked up a stick, to hit something with it.

Obviously, our search for golf's origins has taken us too far. We must retrace our steps and this time see what we can do to define golf more specifically. If golf is taken to be a cross-country club-and-ball game with the ultimate object of putting the ball *into a*

hole, the search is immensely simplified. In that case the claims of Scotland to be the birthplace of golf are enormously strengthened.

In *The Royal and Ancient Game of Golf,* Garden Smith writes rather petulantly: "The poor Scots are denied the possibility of having a game of their own evolved by themselves, in accordance with their own ideas and temperament and suited to their country and climate. How the importation idea arose it is impossible to conceive. The evidence is all against it, but writers on golf have nearly all followed it like sheep."

That little outburst is hardly justified, but even Smith does concede that golf was influenced by the continental games as, of course, it must have been. The close alliance between Scotland and France, with the natural interchange of ideas and people, could not have failed to make its mark on golf. When the first modified rules of golf came to be written they bore such similarities to the rules of *jeu de mail,* almost word for word in places, as to be beyond coincidence.

Having conceded these two debts to the continent, Smith goes on: "There seems to be no reason for doubting that, in all its essential particulars, golf is a purely Scottish product. Apart from the available evidence, literary and pictorial, which is all against a Dutch or other continental origin, the game is characteristically Scottish. It is not Celtic. There are Celts in Scotland, but when we talk of a typical Scot we do not mean a Celt. Golf is certainly not a Celtic game and is, indeed, entirely foreign to the Celtic temperament, which delights in faster and rougher games, such as shinty or football. But anything more typical of the slow, canny, yet strong and resourceful Scottish character than golf is not to be found in the whole range of Scottish institutions. Golf, in fact, in its conception and essence, is the very epitome of the elements which have given the Scottish character its strength and individuality. It is the game of the patient, self-reliant man, prepared to meet whatever fortune may befall him. As the early Scot found life a hard battle, with good and evil fortune mixed capriciously, and only to be won by patience and steadfastness in adverse circumstances, so in his game he sought to reproduce the greater struggle for the smaller stake. He was in no mind to make the game easier or less trying, but rather sought to increase its natural difficulties, recognizing even in his recrea-

Chole as played in France in 1497 (above).
Paintings by Esaias Van de Velde (top l.), Adriaen Van de Velde (top r.), and Aert Van der Neer
depict variations of the Dutch game kolven.

tion, that the harder the struggle, the greater was the joy of mastery."

What wonderful nonsense, all the more nonsensical for that parody of the Scottish character. Slow, canny, strong, patient, resourceful, and steadfast—these are Scottish qualities of the music-hall cliché. They are the characteristics you might cite as circumstantial evidence that the Scots invented an activity like tossing the caber, but they hardly support the theory that the Scots invented golf.

Let us play Smith at his own game and look at those Scottish institutions which reflect that national character according to Smith. We can formulate a persuasive thesis. The architecture fits. It is, above all, stolid. Even the humblest cottage is built with the ponderous simplicity of a stanchion for a bridge, not surprising since the Scots are a race of engineers. No frills, nothing so frivolous as decoration is added. Function is all. The Scottish literary tradition rests almost exclusively on the reputation of novelists whose works are as worthy and nourishing and exciting as haggis. They have produced one poet in a thousand years, and on most people's teams of all-time greats he would not get farther than the substitutes' bench. As for philosophy, the only Scottish contender in the heavyweight division is John Knox, and all he had was a ponderous left hand: "Whatever you are doing, stop it." The Scots, according to the Smith school of thought, excel at the technical pursuits. If you want your appendix removed, or a harbor spanned, or a ship designed, or your books balanced, or an enemy machine-gun post wiped out, you cannot do better than look in the appropriate section of the Yellow Pages under "Mac."

But in the realm of ideas and imagination, on Smith's blueprint of the typical Scot, you would be advised to look to another race, possibly one of those Johnny-come-lately Celts. If the Scots are really so dour, it hardly supports the theory that they invented golf, in the sense of having given birth in a flash of creative inspiration to that paradoxical, diabolically subtle, almost poetical notion of combining the *Donner und Blitz* element of power play with the gossamer delicacy of holing out? Now there's a frivolous embellishment if ever there was one.

Anthropology is a dangerous game. It may be true, in a general sense, that every race is the child of its geology and climate. It does not follow that the Scottish character is all gale-swept granite. People are individuals, and despite Smith's implications to the contrary, a Scot could easily have invented golf, just as a Scot could have written *Hamlet* or composed *The Messiah.*

On the other hand, the probability is that nobody invented golf. Picture for a moment what life was like on the east coast of Scotland at the beginning of the fifteenth century. St. Andrews was a compact fortress town with mean and narrow streets which in those days did duty as drains, rubbish dumps, and sewers. Life was hard. Most of the men clawed a precarious living from the sea or the land, and every arable inch was closely cultivated. The only place to go for recreation was the strip of sand dunes alongside the beach. This sour land could not be cultivated, and all that grew there were hardy whin bushes and a fine turf where sheep grazed. The area performed the function of park, backyard, and social club for the people of St. Andrews. The women brought their washing and draped it over the whins to dry. This was the place for the Sunday walk. Men played football and took their dogs onto the dunes to catch rabbits, and it was here that the compulsory archery practice was held. (Absentees were fined and the money used to buy drink for the regular attenders, a splendid example of the common sense which runs so strongly through the Scottish judicial processes.)

If any form of outdoor game was to be played, this was the only place to go. If some returning soldier did interest his friends in chole or kolven,

41

In "St. Nicholas's Day" by Jan Steen, gift of a kolven club to one young lad seems to have caused a certain amount of disappointment to less fortunate sibling on the left.

they would have to go out to the links. Of if a traveler came with the news of some native sport played with clubs and ball, possibly from Ireland, the story would be the same. As we have seen, at that time there was nothing original about club-and-ball games. We may presume, at all events, that at some stage a band of pioneers advanced on the links armed with clubs and balls, either at St. Andrews itself or some place like it along this stretch of coastline.

Now, how should they proceed? The lie of the land would dictate their route. They would naturally follow the smooth valleys between the dunes, skirting such obstructions as the archery range and the washing. But what should they aim at? On this bleak landscape, with no trees or convenient church doors to play to, the only natural landmarks which would stand out clearly would be rabbit holes. It might have been planned beforehand to use a hole as a target, but the probability is that it all happened by fortuitous accident. The peculiar nature of the links surely dictated the form of golf. It might have been an act of individual inspiration, but that theory looks, on the face of it, unlikely. A Scot might have invented golf; more probably Scotland invented golf.

It is a point of academic interest only, except in one particular. The administrators of golf are concerned, and rightly so, with preserving the game as nearly as possible in its original form, and if the rabbit was indeed the original greenkeeper, then the hole into which we frustrated golfers try to aim our putts in this twentieth century ought, for the sake of tradition if nothing else, to be rather more generous in diameter than four and a quarter inches. Many people believe that there is a disproportionate emphasis on putting in the modern game. They claim that the balance of golf has swung too much in favor of the specialist putter and that a six-inch hole would restore the importance of shot-making. They have logic on their side, and, if the rabbit-hole theory is true, they have an ally in tradition.

In this 17th-century painting of chole players by the Flemish artist Paul Bril, door at left serves as target. Note length of the clubs, size of the ball.

That argument must be pleaded at another time in another place. For the moment we must return to medieval Scotland and to fact rather than fancy. And the fact is that, whatever its genesis, golf captured the public imagination so strongly that eventually it threatened national security. Men neglected their archery for the new sport. And in spite of the decrees outlawing the game—or possibly because of the added spice of illegality—golf flourished.

At the beginning of the new century, a treaty of perpetual peace was signed between England and Scotland. The optimism of this document may not have been entirely justified by subsequent events, but by and large the heat was off. It was no longer necessary to keep armies in readiness for war and the way was open for golf to develop and spread.

Shall we shed a tear for the men who made bows and arrows and who now, in these peaceful times, found themselves in a falling market? Not at all. One reason for the spread of golf was that the game inherited a ready-made industry to service it. The bowyers and fletchers were craftsmen wise in the properties of native woods and skilled in the arts of turning and balancing shafts and forging iron. A man who could shape the arrow for a longbow or a crossbow's bolt had at hand the tools and skills to make golf clubs. Who better than a bowyer to know about the flex and torsion of a blackthorn bough, or the security to be found in a rawhide grip?

They turned naturally to clubmaking as a profitable sideline and golf's debt to archery has never been properly appreciated and acknowledged. If golf had relied on the rude agricultural implements used for kolven the game would surely never have achieved such popularity. By later standards, when clubmaking became a highly developed art, the early clubs may have seemed crude but at least they proved effective.

For something like two hundred years after that first proclamation outlawing golf the game

44

THE PENNY MAGAZINE

OF THE

Society for the Diffusion of Useful Knowledge.

181.]   PUBLISHED EVERY SATURDAY.   [JANUARY 31, 1835.

THE GAME OF SHINTY

[Game of Shinty.]

In the Highlands of Scotland it is customary for persons to amuse themselves, in the winter season, with a game which they call " shinty." This sport has a considerable resemblance to that which is denominated " hurling " in England, and which Strutt describes under that name. The shinty is played with a small hard ball, which is generally made of wood, and each player is furnished with a curved stick somewhat resembling that which is used by golf players. The object of each party of players is to send the ball beyond a given boundary on either side; and the skill of the game consists in striking the ball to the greatest distance towards the adversaries' boundary, or in manœuvring to keep it in advance of the opposing side. Large parties assemble during the Christmas holidays, one parish sometimes making a match against another. In the struggles between the contending players many hard blows are given, and frequently a shin is broken, or by a rarer chance some more serious accident may occur. The writer witnessed a match, in which one of the players, having gained possession of the ball, contrived to run a mile with it in his hand, pursued by both his own and the adverse party until he reached the appointed limit, when his victory was admitted. Many of the Highland farmers join with eagerness in the sport, and the laird frequently encourages by his presence this amusement of his labourers and tenants.

"Kolf Player" by H. Brown from 1841
De Nederlanden and illustration of the organized mayhem
known in Scotland and Ireland as "shinty"
are extreme examples of alleged parentage of golf.

Summer kolven—in winter it was played on ice—from
Flemish Book of Hours of 1530. Stained glass window (r.)
of Gloucester cathedral is earliest pictorial evidence
(mid-14th century) of golf in England. (Detail, upper r.)

was an informal affair. There were no codified rules, although no doubt there were conventions on how the game should be played, probably varying from one community to another. (This is another reason for doubting whether the distinction of having invented golf can ever be ascribed to an individual. The game had been evolving for three hundred years before it achieved anything like a standardized form.) There were no set "courses" as we know them today; you simply played over whatever suitable ground happened to be available, cutting holes where necessary with a pocket knife.

The game went through vicissitudes, at times being repressed by decrees forbidding it on Sundays, sometimes being encouraged by royal patronage. Most of the Scottish kings were golfers and poor Mary Queen of Scots was accused of callously playing golf immediately after the murder of her husband. For the keen student of the history of golf it is a fascinating period, with a wealth of documented evidence, but the next significant change did not occur until the early part of the seventeenth century with the introduction of the feather ball, or "featherie."

At its best, the featherie must have represented a considerable improvement on the earlier balls of turned boxwood. Its irregular surface pattern would have given it far better flight characteristics. Distance records are unreliable because one can never be quite sure what the conditions were like at the time but, taking a cautious average from contemporary accounts, it is clear that a good player could drive a featherie 200 yards. And in 1836, a French schoolmaster at St. Andrews, on a frosty Old Course and with a gentle following wind, hit a measured drive of 361 yards. In wet weather the featherie was not nearly so effective since it absorbed water and became heavy and soggy. And, of course, one injudicious blow with the sharp edge of an iron club was liable to split the cover and disembowel this expensive missile.

The featherie was made by the same process employed by the Romans. A cover of untanned bull's hide was stitched, leaving a small aperture so that it could then be turned inside out, with the raised seams inside, and stuffed with boiled feathers—traditionally, enough to fill a top hat. The aperture was then stitched shut and the ball pounded into shape. As the feathers dried they expanded to make a hard, resilient ball, ready for painting. It was a skilled operation to make a featherie and a craftsman was doing well if he turned out half a dozen a day.

Compared with the earlier boxwood balls, the featheries were prohibitively expensive, costing twelve times as much, and this inflationary move was reflected in a social change in the game. Golf became a luxury, and although the Scots managed to keep the classless tradition of the game alive, the situation was very different in the game's missionary fields. The golf which spread to England early in the seventeenth century, largely through the enthusiasm of her Scottish-born king, James I, was most definitely a game for the nobility. The idea of golf as a pursuit of the well-born and wealthy proved to be enduring and damaging to the development of the game. Even today, three hundred years later, when the talk at the pit face among coal miners is just as likely to concern how they scored in the monthly medal competition, the notion persists in some quarters that golf is a game of the privileged minority. In England, local authorities of a socialist bias still refuse to consider the provision of municipal golf courses on the grounds that public money should not be spent on amenities for "toffs."

If the featherie must take initial responsibility for this state of affairs, it also advanced the game considerably. The improvements arose not only through the superior properties of the ball itself, but because of the new challenge it offered to the clubmaker. Whereas a club which had to withstand constant impact with unyielding wooden balls had of necessity to

be of sturdy construction, the featherie presented opportunities for refinement. From this time the craft of clubmaking developed into an art.

The oldest surviving clubs date from the seventeenth century and provide some evidence of what golf was like in the early days. The set consists of six woods and two irons, which confirms the theory of the historical development of golf. Probably in the very beginning golf was played with a single wooden club. Then variations were introduced to deal with specific situations. One such would be the baffing spoon. The original play club (later called the driver) would have served its purpose well enough when the ball was teed up on a pinch of sand. But the straight-faced play club would have been ineffective from a tight fairway lie. Hence, the introduction of a club with

an angled face and the technique of baffing, or bouncing the clubhead into the turf just behind the ball to make it rise. From that point we may surmise the introduction of further variations, such as the long spoon and the holing-out club, or putter. The seventeenth-century set marks the transitional period when iron clubs were becoming popular and the proliferation of woods began to decline. It gives an impression of size and crudeness. Each is about six inches longer than the equivalent club of today. The heads are deeper and more heavily weighted. In every case the face is slightly concave, presumably in an attempt to impart control. This hollowing of the face, combined with the name "spoon," may give us a clue to the method of using the clubs. The inference is that the ball was spooned, with a scooping action, which would tally with the club's

49

general dimensions. Anything in the nature of a "hit" would be impossible with implements of this weight and size. Restoration golfers would most certainly have had to "wait for it" as those great, weighted heads built up a ponderous speed on the periphery of their wide arc. These clubs would need to be swung with a lazy, sweeping action, probably embellished by a dipping or scooping motion in the contact zone. As to the outcome of the shot, we can only apply our modern knowledge of aerodynamics and insist that the balls must have been roughened in some way to produce an approximately true flight path. In constant play any ball, whether of boxwood or bullhide with feather interior, would become scuffed, and we do know that the tradi-

tion arose of the need for golf balls to "mature."

We should not assume that, simply because the equipment was crude by modern standards, it was many times less effective. As soon as authenticated records appear we find surprisingly good results being recorded. The laws of dynamics have not changed over the ages and the distance a ball may be struck was governed in the seventeenth century by the same forces that govern it today: the size, density, and resilience of the ball combined with the mass and speed of the clubhead. The resilience of the ball would have been inferior, but if it were smaller and heavier than today's artificially regulated examples the overall difference might well have been small.

The other fundamental change, the use of the steel shaft, does not make the slightest difference in the speed of the clubhead. It is vastly more convenient, and it makes the task of swinging a club somewhat easier, but a modern set of irons could be fitted with wooden shafts without altering their performance in the slightest degree. So, if we assume that these early golfers mastered a technique of extracting the maximum theoretical performance from their clubs —and the continued popularity of the game suggests at the very least that golf for them was a highly satisfying pastime—we must suppose that they hit a proportion of shots which were good by any yardstick. Of necessity, it would be low-trajectory golf, since their

equipment simply would not produce the high-soaring modern shot. But on hard, unwatered linksland a low shot which pitches and runs is often the most effective, especially in windy conditions.

We may, in summary, rest assured that this early golf was, at its highest levels, considerably more refined than the popular notion of bumbling the ball along the ground in hundred-yard stages. At the same time, looking at those hollowed faces with the knowledge that even the finest of contemporary professionals does not strike every shot exactly off the "meat," we must accept that the perfect shot was a somewhat rarer occurrence in the seventeenth century than it is today. They must have had plenty of foozles

Trendy sportswear for the links as favored by the younger set of 17th-century Holland and gentlemen golfers of Scotland at the beginning of the nineteenth century.

in every round. No wonder they drank such prodigious quantities of alcohol afterwards.

Incidentally, although the use of numbers to distinguish clubs may be appropriate to this computer age, golf surely has been impoverished by the loss of those wonderful Scottish names for clubs. Dull of soul is he who feels no difference between a five-iron and, as it once was called, a mashie. The driver retains its name, although of comparatively recent origin (being the successor to the play club). The wedge (much more recent) continues to resist attempts to submerge its individuality in the No. 10. And the putter defies the passion for numerology, which is only proper since of all the clubs it is the most personal—indeed, in temperament the most human. There would be little satisfaction in breaking a No. 11 across your knee, and the love-hate relationship most golfers enjoy with their putters could scarcely survive the substitution of an anonymous number. But the brassie and spoon are disappearing from the language of golf while cleek, baffie, mashie, and niblick have already vanished.

For tournament professionals golf has become a science rather than an art and for them numbered clubs may be appropriate. But club golfers who play the game for pleasure, and for whom aesthetic considerations are half the charm of the game, would surely get satisfaction from a revival of those wonderful names. Those soulless businessmen who mass-produce matched sets and are concerned with balance sheets rather than traditions, say that numbers are necessary because there are not enough names to go round. What they overlook, because it suits their pockets, is that the average golfer does not need fourteen clubs and is quite incapable of benefiting from such a range.

In the hands of a powerful pro a four-iron will hit the ball 15 yards farther than a five-iron. For a handicap golfer this differential comes down to 10 yards. However, the average amateur is not consistent enough to exploit that small difference. His well-hit five-iron goes farther than his indifferent four-iron shot. For him—and he represents well over ninety percent of the world's golfers—a set of irons graduated according to the modern scale, that is, a three, four and a half, six, seven and a half, and nine, would adequately cater to his needs. In other words, cleek, mashie, mid-iron, mashie-niblick, and niblick. Add a driver, brassie, and spoon with lofts equivalent to one-wood, two-and-a-half-wood, and four-wood, plus a sand iron, wedge, and putter, and he has a set of eleven clubs, which is two more than Harry Vardon needed to win his six Open Championships.

Quite apart from the considerable financial saving such a set would represent and the added pleasure the player would find in his named clubs, the game itself might well become more enjoyable by bringing back the need to "invent" half-shots, cut-ups, and the "feel" strokes. Golf's appeal lies in the combination of power and artistry. In this brutal golfing age anything which tends to emphasize the artistry is to be encouraged. However, we dupes allow ourselves to be persuaded that fourteen clubs constitute a "set," and that unless we are equipped like Jack Nicklaus we cannot hope to play like him. The premise is as absurd as the aspiration.

After the formation of proper clubs, a process that began around 1740, the next significant development in golf was the standardization of courses and rules. This was the period when golf ceased to be a happy-go-luck activity and formality entered into the game. Nowadays golfers who travel around the countryside like to tell each other, "What a place this would be to build a golf course." In those early days that thought was enough. If you had clubs and balls to hand you played wherever you found a piece of suitable country. In Scotland the golfing grounds were of necessity the common lands, but when we read of royal personages playing golf in the royal park at Greenwich,

Early styles of golf. Drawing probably uses some artistic license but the meticulous painting gives historical weight to the larger-hole protagonists.

it does not mean a golf course was there.

The earliest references to stroke play date from this era in the middle of the eighteenth century, as does the earliest surviving code of rules. It is interesting to note that our ancestors managed to get along on thirteen brief laws, compared with the present proliferation of forty-one, many of them divided into numerous subclauses, definitions, appendices, and instructions on etiquette.

Although the game was in a fairly advanced state of development, there still was no such thing as a formalized golf course as we know it today. At one of the earliest links, for instance, at Leith, near Edinburgh, the game was played over five holes measuring 414, 461, 426, 495, and 435 yards. If these distances are adjusted for the equipment of the day, they are the equivalent of about 600 yards for each hole, good three-shotters for the best players. Here again we have direct evidence to refute the modern view that putting is half of golf. Nowadays, on a par-72 course, the first-class golfer is allowed a "ration" of two putts a hole, thirty-six in all. The ratio of shots through the green to putts in the days when Leith was a five-hole course must have been nearer two to one. A round at Leith probably consisted of three circuits, so there could be no basis for comparison with the golfers of, say,

Perth, whose course had six holes, or Montrose, which had twenty-five.

In any case, stroke-play golf with card and pencil had not yet become popular. Golf was mainly man-to-man encounters, blood-and-guts matches with all the interest of private wagers and the interplay of personality. Those of the generation reared on a diet of almost unrelieved match play tend to regard it as the "real" golf, and find stroke play insipid stuff by comparison. In this respect at least we must concede that the traditionalists are right. One of the regrettable trends of modern times is the decline of match play, following the pervasive example of the professional tournaments with their necessary emphasis on scores.

Whether or not the first golf was played at St. Andrews, the city of Edinburgh must be given credit for forming the first club. In 1744 a group of "honorable gentlemen golfers" petitioned the city fathers to provide a silver club for open competition among the golfing community. The trophy was duly provided and the championship announced by proclamation and tuck of drum. Twenty years later the Honourable Company of Edinburgh Golfers was formally constituted as a club, although it had no clubhouse, nor indeed did it own the golfing grounds at Leith. Nevertheless, minute books were kept of the club's activities

St. Andrews was (and is) golf's Mecca. Preceding pages: 1850
Grand Match, painted by Charles Lee, is a group
portrait; girl serving ginger beer symbolizes the 15th, or Ginger
Beer, hole. Above: Old Tom Morris on first tee, 1895.

and from such records we can get an accurate picture of the golfing way of life of those days.

Let us take a typical Saturday in, say, 1780, when the club tradition was well established, and follow the movements of a prosperous merchant. The only paid official of the club was a boy whose job was to call on every member and inquire if he proposed to dine with the club on Saturday. Having given due notice of his intention to be present at dinner (cost: one shilling) the merchant would dress in his scarlet club uniform with crested buttons, and call for his carriage to take him to his appointment on the links. There he would meet his prearranged opponent, possibly a surgeon or an officer from the castle garrison, and their regular caddies. These caddies, probably reeking and fuddled from their ale-house excesses of the previous night, would take their owners' clubs in a bundle under their arms and play could begin. Undoubtedly it would be a match, and after pinching up

a small pyramid of loose sand, the golfers would tee their balls and strike off with their play clubs.

The sight of these two splendid creatures in their finery would certainly attract a gallery of casual strollers, and the caddies would be kept busy clearing picnic parties and dog-walkers from the path of the match. By all accounts the caddies would not be too particular about the language they employed in their control of the public. For all their faults, the caddies were fiercely partisan and jealously protected the rights of their masters. The tradition among caddies of knowing how to milk a fat tip is as old as golf itself. On one occasion, when a spectator was crowding the hole so closely that he impeded the player's stroke, the caddie grabbed the onlooker by the back of the neck and thrust his nose into the hole with the words: "There now! You can see the ball's in the hole right enough."

After the game the serious business of

Lining it up: Formidable professional partnership of Allan Robertson (bending) and Tom Morris in a match at St. Andrews, 1849, and a daintier scene of the ladies of Westward Ho!, Devon.

Those were the days, before the First World War, when
life was leisurely—at Baltusrol, New Jersey,
(above) and at St. Andrews (top r.)—and Walter
Travis (opposite) was a power in golf.

the club would begin. The golfers would change into their dining uniforms, possibly blue or gray coats with black facings and gilt buttons, and repair to a private room in a local tavern for dinner, presided over by the Captain (an office automatically assumed by the winner of the club championship). It was customary for members to provide food from their own estates, and these golfers did themselves well. Club minutes recall feasts of a round of beef stewed in hock, haunch of venison, saddle of mutton, reindeer's tongue, pigeon pie, and sheep's-head pasty. The Royal Aberdeen club accounts show an average consumption in excess of three bottles of liquor per man at their dinners, and Tobias Smollett writes of the club golfer customarily

retiring with a gallon of claret in his belly. The business of the club was transacted during the meal. A member who had been observed playing golf out of uniform might be fined half a dozen bottles of rum or Highland whisky. And then the wagers would be recorded. This ritual was the normal method of organizing matches for the following week. One member might challenge another to a match for a gallon of whisky and the details would duly be recorded in the book. At the same time, from reference to the previous week's entries, settlement would be demanded for that day's results. Since booze in some form was the common currency of golf wagers and payment was exacted at dinner, we can imagine that late in the

Golf began to change, with players like young Walter
Hagen breaking through and equipment improving from the featherie
(opposite, top) to the gutties (dark ball and starred ball below
it), and early rubber-cores, including 1899 Haskell (top r.).

62

evening some imprudent challenges were made. Never mind. It was an age of high conviviality and good fellowship; golf was not the solemn affair it later became. And the morrow was a day of rest.

Two fortuitous events combined to shape the future course of the game. First, the golfers of St. Andrews achieved the reputation of being the pacesetters and unofficial authorities on the game, largely as the result of what the historian, Dr. Young, describes as a tourist promotion stunt. The Society of St. Andrews golfers put up a trophy in the form of a silver club for open competition. The success of this contest established St. Andrews as the premier golfing town, and when, in 1764, the Society changed its course from twelve holes to eighteen, other clubs followed suit. Hence, eighteen holes became the "correct" number for a full course.

New courses naturally were built to the St. Andrews pattern. Previously, the St. Andrews golfers had twelve holes, playing eleven going out and then retracing their steps and playing eleven holes home, over the same fairways in reverse direction. A "round" was thus twenty-two holes. Then the Society decided to turn the first four holes into two and the round was thereby reduced to eighteen.

Other clubs did not follow the famous St. Andrews practice of shared fairways and greens, because this was essentially dictated by the narrow strip of duneland available. In any case, greens—in the sense of large areas of carefully prepared turf—were unknown. The practice was to tee up your ball within a club's length of the hole just completed. If putting was not so important in those eighteenth-century days, it must have been an even more tiresome process than it is on today's superbly groomed carpets.

The first reference to golf in America was the formation of the South Carolina Golf Club at Charleston, around 1786. The Scottish transplant did not long survive on the alien soil of the New World,

however, and another hundred years passed before the game was reintroduced to the United States, this time to stay. By then, it had made considerable progress. The Society of St. Andrews golfers was dignified by William IV (1830-37) with the title of "Royal and Ancient" and the era of championships had begun, first the Amateur and then the Open, which began as a thirty-six hole professional tournament for a championship belt. Even more significantly, perhaps, in the mid-1800s was another happy accident, the invention of the gutta-percha ball, or guttie. A professor at St. Andrews University, so the legend goes, received a statue of Vishnu which had been packed in gutta-percha for protection. This rubber-like substance is tapped from a tree and turns hard on exposure to the air. The professor, a keen golfer, idly rolled a piece of it into a ball. (It must have been heated to reach this degree of malleability, but let us not spoil a harmless legend for the sake of a technical detail.) He wondered whether golf could be played with his gutta-percha ball, tried it out, and failed to achieve anything better than bumbling shots along the ground. It takes more than a minor setback to deter a true Scot inspired by the vision of saving a few pence, however. He persevered and in time, as the gutta-percha ball became scuffed by the battering of the clubhead, it began to fly. The reason, as we now know, is that a golf ball obtains lift from its dimples. It is an aerodynamic necessity to have an irregular surface; a perfectly smooth ball has no lift. And so, after more trial and error, the guttie came to golf. At first, its surface irregularities were hammered by hand, but later the guttie was produced in molds and many novel surface designs were tried to produce better performance, such as an imitation of a feather ball's stitched seam, a bramble pattern, and a lattice formation.

The guttie had several advantages. It was cheap, and when it became misshapen or chipped, it could be plunged into hot water and remolded. There was some resistance to the new ball, especially from the professionals whose ballmaking activities were a profitable sideline. Their opposition could not long hold up progress, for progress this certainly was. The cost of golf, after the initial capital expense of clubs, was now reasonable again, and the game was ready for its second era of expansion.

The British empire was serviced by expatriates, many of them Scots, and golf followed the flag. Clubs were formed in imperial outposts. And it was reintroduced into the U.S. in 1888. This time the game clicked. Although the guttie ball lasted for only sixty years, this was perhaps the most important period in the history of golf. For between 1850 and 1900 golf became truly international. The beachheads were established from which golf was to enslave the world.

Another effect of the guttie was that the clubmakers again had to make adjustments for this stone-like ball. Wooden clubs designed for use with the featherie could not be expected to withstand the impact shock of the unyielding guttie. At first they tried facing the clubs with patches of leather, which served to absorb some of the initial shock but also reduced the effectiveness of the shot, especially in bad weather. They then turned to new hardwoods for the clubheads, and the design of the heads themselves evolved by stages from the graceful banana shapes of the traditional design into the rounder forms which, with variations, are used today.

Most writers who review the history of golf tend to see the development of the game in terms of eras and, indeed, in this chapter an attempt has been made to isolate the significant changes which altered the course of the game and guided its destiny. The difficulty is to determine which were the decisive influences. For instance, there comes a point when golf in America ceased to be an offshoot of a foreign game and flowered in a uniquely American way. The child began to dominate the parent.

Obviously, it was a developing process over a period of twenty years or so, and the problem is to fix a date for the era. Should it be from the first major American contribution to golf (Walter Travis's victory in the 1904 Amateur Championship at Sandwich)? Or should it be from the time when American golfers were established beyond argument as leaders of the world (Walter Hagen's 1922 Open triumph)? Since the game has so often been shaped by changes in equipment, as we have seen, perhaps the date of another and far-reaching technical development is an appropriate moment to select as heralding the coming era of American domination.

In 1901, a Cleveland chemist, Coburn Haskell, invented a method of making golf balls by winding rubber thread under tension around a central core. Others had tried to use rubber for golf balls, and a composition ball, made to a secret formula which certainly used rubber, had enjoyed limited success; the "puttie" as it was called, might have developed into a popular substitute for the guttie, but Haskell's ball was so obviously superior that it quickly ousted all rivals. This invention, America's first significant contribution to golf, followed the formation seven years previously of the United States Golf Association. Incidentally, the Royal and Ancient Golf Club of St. Andrews, although the acknowledged authority for golf and its rules, was not invested with the management of the Open and Amateur Championships until 1919, so, in this respect at least, the R. and A. is junior to the USGA.

Within the space of eighteen years, Walter Travis beat the British in their Amateur Championship, Francis Ouimet beat the best of the overseas challengers to win the U.S. Open, and Walter Hagen recorded the first of a long succession of American victories in the British Open Championship. The game which had started as an informal knock-about on the sandy turf of a Scottish fishing town four hundred and fifty years previously was now full grown and under new management.

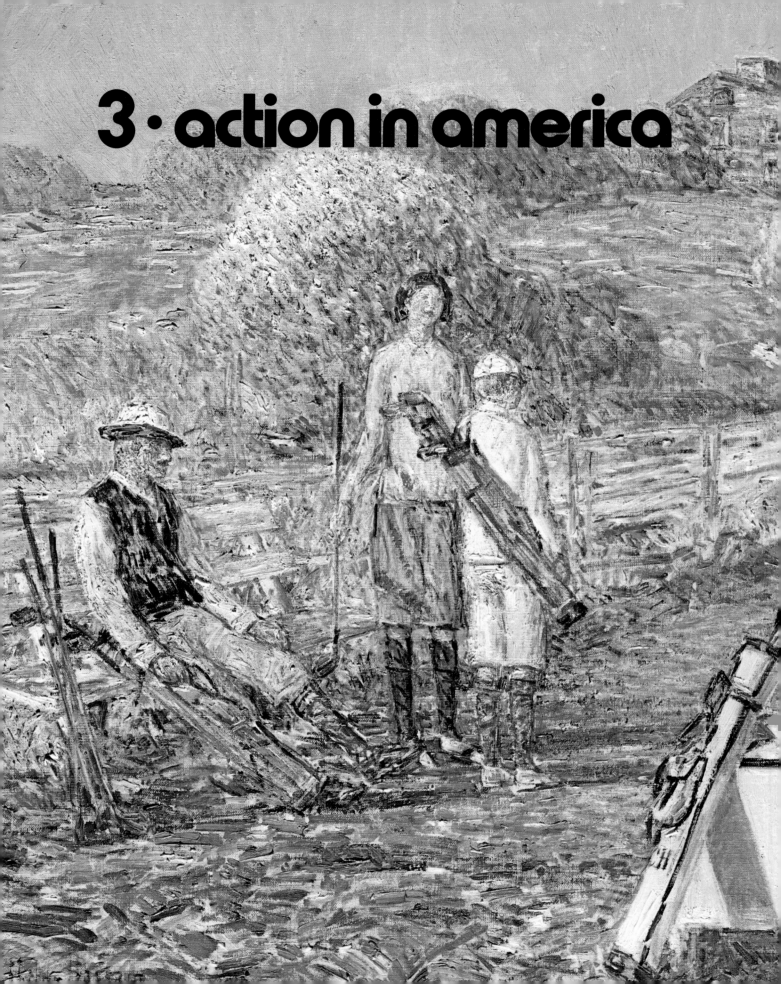

3 · action in america

Perhaps the most teasing problem facing the historian of American golf is to determine how and where and when the game first came to be played in the United States. The question, however, is of purely academic interest, because although there are a number of references to golf dating from the middle of the seventeenth century, it is equally clear that the game did not survive at that time.

Of that first introduction of golf to America we know very little, and there is even some doubt whether those earliest references applied to the Scottish game at all. The evidence suggests that the Dutch game of kolven was played by the settlers of New Netherlands and it was probably this game, not golf, which earned the displeasure of the magistrates at Fort Orange in 1657. Once again, as in Scotland, the first evidence of a golfing game is found in official attempts to outlaw the pastime.

A number of tantalizing references to golf between 1779 and 1812 have survived. What are we to make of an advertisement, for instance, which appeared in *Rivington's Royal Gazette* in New York on April 21, 1779?

TO THE GOLF PLAYERS
The Season for this pleasant and healthful
Exercise now advancing, Gentlemen may be furnished
with excellent CLUBS and the veritable Caledonian
BALLS, by enquiring at the Printers.

This notice had nothing to do with kolven. Since Rivington was an importer and merchant, as well as printer, he may have shipped in some equipment for Scottish officers and found himself with some surplus clubs and balls on his hands.

The Savannah (Georgia) Golf Club today proudly displays a framed invitation of 1811 which reads:

GOLF CLUB BALL
The Honor of Miss Eliza Johnston's company
is requested to a Ball to be given by the Members
of the Golf Club of this city, at the Exchange,
on Tuesday evening the 13th instant,
at 7 o'clock.

Here we have proof of the existence of a golf club, but no golf relics have survived from those days, and no references have been discovered to prove that the members actually played Caledonian golf. Perhaps they did. If not, we are left with the charming theory that the good people of Savannah had copied the social aspect of Scottish clubs, with their emphasis on dining and conviviality, and simply adopted the word "Golf" as a title. Possibly the members consumed their regulation gallons of claret and sides of beef without bothering themselves with the tedious ritual of hacking a ball around the countryside.

Subsequently, the records make it clear that both golf and kolven were established as distinctly separate sports, with clubs devoted to each game, by the end of the eighteenth century. If South Carolina and Georgia were indeed the early strongholds of golf, it is interesting to note that when the game was reintroduced a hundred years later these areas again flourished as golfing centers.

Golf disappeared from public record with the war against Great Britain in 1812, and the next significant development took place in 1887, when a Scot, Robert Lockhart, imported half a dozen clubs and a quantity of guttie balls. His friend John Reid of Yonkers was intrigued by Lockhart's stories of golf and decided to try the game for himself. Reid interested some friends and they had a three-hole course laid out in a meadow near Reid's home. Was this the first American golf club?

Let us pause and consider the social scene. By the time golf returned to America the nation had

Preceding pages: Childe Hassam's "Mixed Foursome,"
painted in 1923, shows first tee of
the Maidstone club on Long Island. Father, at left,
may have hooked one out-of-bounds.

changed greatly. The political union had been accompanied by an ethnic fusion. Whereas the first American golf had been played by transplanted Europeans, the second golfing invasion was made on a country whose people saw themselves as citizens of a new nation. Instead of a country fragmented into colonies of exiles, America was now inhabited by Americans. So we cannot say that golf was introduced to America when Lockhart and Scottish-born merchants began to amuse themselves by hitting golf balls around a New York meadow, but we can assert with confidence that golf had truly arrived in America when John Reid and his native-born friends took up the game.

In fact, a group of Scots who formed the Oakhurst Golf Club in West Virginia have a stronger claim to the honor of being the first of the modern American golfers by a year or so, but the Yonkers players deserve most of the missionary credit. Reid and his friends formed themselves into The St. Andrews Golf Club at Yonkers-on-Hudson in 1888, and when they moved four years later to an apple orchard, with six holes, the club became known as "the Apple-Tree Gang."

The sportswriter, O. B. Keeler, who was best known as the traveling companion and biographer of Bobby Jones, wrote that the Apple-Tree Gang laid out their lunch behind the 6th green, where bar service was dispensed from a wicker-covered demijohn of whisky. By tradition, the holes at the Merion Golf Club near Philadelphia, one of the earliest clubs in the country, are marked not by flags, but by sticks topped with wicker baskets. No one knows the origin of the baskets of Merion, but it is possible that they hark back to the Apple-Tree Gang. After all, it would be quite logical for the Yonkers players to impale their empty bottles on sticks to mark the holes. And what could be more natural than for the founding fathers of Merion to follow suit? Stranger things happened in those formative years, when no one knew exactly how to set about this

odd game. (Th[...]
veals that whe[...]
its course on [...]
apple trees w[...]
of the game.)

could have de[...]
offered by th[...]
24, 1889, had ever gained favor. As described in a syndicated article by a special correspondent, golf was "a popular Scottish pastime which affords lots of excitement." A subhead explained further that "No dude can play it because brawn and vigor are essential qualities. The players have servants and sometimes run many miles—spectators in the way."

The article, in part, read as follows:

"Given a strong pair of lungs, firm muscles upon the legs and a healthy desire to emulate others in physical exercise, a man may become a golf player. Without these he had better stay out of the sport, for no man who cannot run several miles without stopping can make any kind of a respectable appearance in the game.

"In addition to the fact that it appeals to men of athletic development, it is also by the nature of the game itself, a most aristocratic exercise; for no man can play at golf who has not a servant at command to assist him. The truth is that the servant is as essential to the success of the game as the player himself. Perhaps the best description of the game, which would certainly be unique in a republic, may be given in the words of one of the most expert players in this vicinity, Mr. Alexander D. MacFarlane.

" 'To play golf properly we need a very large expanse of uncultivated soil, which is not too much broken up by hills. . . . Having selected a field, the first thing necessary is to dig a small hole perhaps one foot or two feet deep and about four inches in diameter. Beginning with this hole, a circle is devised that in-

cludes substantially the whole of the links. About once in 500 yards of this circle a hole is dug corresponding to the one I have just described. The design is to make as large a circle as possible, with holes at about the same distance apart.

       " 'The game then may be played, with two or four persons. If by four, two of them must be upon the same side. There are eleven implements of the game, most important of which is the ball. This is made of gutta-percha and is painted white. It weighs about two ounces and is just small enough to fit comfortably into the holes dug in the ground. Still it should not be so large that it cannot be taken out with ease. The other ten implements are the tools of the players. They are of

various shapes as may be inferred from the names of the implements. The spoon, for instance, is a rough approximation to what we generally understand as a spoon and is designed to lift the ball out of holes, or sinks, in the ground. The club, of course, is simply an instrument with which to bat the ball. The same practically applies to the driving putter. All these implements of the game are designed to fit into the various situations in which the player may find himself.

       " 'At the beginning of play each player places his ball at the edge of a hole which has been designated as a starting point. When the word has been given to start, he bats his ball as accurately as possible toward the next hole, which may be, as I have said,

Earliest photo (1888) of golf in America is of St. Andrews club's pasture course (top l.) before move to the orchard (l.) which gave members the "Apple-Tree Gang" nickname. Above: Course construction when horsepower meant horses.

Growing boom of golf was reflected in 1901 advertising and in some ludicrous attempts (opposite) to explain the game to newspaper readers of America in 1889.

either 100 or 500 yards distant. As soon as it is started in the air he runs forward in the direction which the ball has taken and his servant, who is called a "caddy" runs after him with all the other nine tools in his arms. If the player is expert or lucky, he bats his ball so that it falls within a few feet or inches, even, of the next hole in the circle. His purpose is to put the ball into that next hole, spoon it out and drive it forward to the next further one before his opponent can accomplish the same end. The province of the "caddy" in the game is to follow his master as closely as possible, generally at a dead run, and be ready to hand him whichever implement of the game the master calls for, as the play may demand. For instance, the ball may fall in such a way that it is lodged an inch or two above the ground, having fallen in thick grass. The player rushing up to it would naturally call upon his "caddy" for a baffing spoon and, having received it from the hands of his servant, he would bat the ball with the spoon in the direction of the next hole.

"'You can see that in this the "caddy" really gets about as much exercise out of the sport as his master, and he must be so familiar with the tools of the game that he can hand out the right implement at any moment when it is called for. If a player has succeeded in throwing or pushing his ball into a hole, his opponent must wait until he has succeeded in spooning it out before he begins to play. Obedience to this rule obviates any dispute as to the order in which a man's points are to be made. For if I have my ball in a hole and my opponent has his within an inch or two of it, he must wait before he plays until I have gotten my ball clear of it and thrown it towards the next hole. Following this general plan the players go entirely about the circle, and, as you may see, in a large field it may involve a run of several miles. If I should throw my ball beyond the hole at which I must next enter, I am obliged to knock it back until it shall enter the desired place and be carefully spooned out again. While I am doing

72

Waiting for the Word

Scoring at a Hole

Player and Assistant

Playing Well Together

Where the Spoon Is Handy

The American tradition was born—with resort golf at Long Beach and the palatial standard set by Stanford White's 1892 design for first U.S. clubhouse, at the Shinnecock Hills Country Club.

74

this my opponent may by a lucky play get his ball within the proper limit and thus gain some distance on me.' "

What a pity that America did not respond to the idea of such a healthy sport! It is interesting to speculate how this special correspondent managed to get quite such a garbled picture of golf. Clearly he had never seen the game played; perhaps the most charitable explanation is that the article arose from a chance meeting in a bar with Mr. Alexander D. MacFarlane, and that they both made a night of it.

The glorious absurdity of the MacFarlane version will be appreciated by anyone with the slightest acquaintance with golf. At the same time, it must be admitted, the formative years of American golf did involve some eccentricities hardly less credible than the fantasies of Mr. MacFarlane and his amanuensis.

In a situation of snowballing popularity for a game about which few Americans had any real knowledge, there was ample scope for scoundrels. Two men who did much to misdirect those first halting footsteps of American golf are worthy of mention. According to American golf writer Charles Price, one of the villains was Tom Bendelow, who worked as a compositor on a New York newspaper.

Bendelow was a Scot and although Americans had great difficulty understanding his accent, they assumed he knew what he was talking about. Actually, his knowledge of golf was of the sketchiest, but he realized that he was ahead of the market. He talked himself into a job as an architectural consultant. Price's description cannot be improved: "Bendelow's methods were simple, to say the least. As an appropriate spot he would mark the first tee with a stake. Then he would pace off a hundred yards and stake off that spot with a simple cross bunker. Then he would march another hundred yards and mark this location for a mound that was to be built in the shape of a chocolate drop. Then he would walk another hundred yards, more or less, and mark the location for a green. All of Bendelow's

greens assumed one of two shapes: perfectly round or perfectly square. None of the greens was protected by hazards, most of them were indistinguishably flat, and all of them had to be ploughed under within a few years because, as anyone with a smattering of agronomy could see, they were nothing more than weed nurseries."

Bendelow could lay out a course in one day, for a $25 fee, and he managed to perpetrate more than six hundred monstrosities.

The other notable rascal of the day was of a very different breed. Charles Blair Macdonald was a big man in every way. He had a large physique and a large voice, a large personality, and a large opinion of himself. Unlike most Americans, he had a thorough knowledge of golf from his years as a student at St. Andrews University and he was a considerable player. Who better than Macdonald, then, to ensure that championship golf in America was organized on a sound basis? That, at any rate, was Macdonald's opinion when he failed to win an invitational tournament over thirty-six holes of stroke play organized by the Newport Golf Club. Macdonald roared his objections, including the complaint that it was absurd to consider a stroke-play competition as an amateur championship. Nobody knew what was correct. Later the St. Andrews Club organized a match-play tournament. Again Macdonald was beaten, albeit in the final and in the aftermath of an injudicious bottle of champagne over lunch. And again Macdonald ranted that this was not a proper championship, his main argument resting on the fact that he had not won it. At least the farcical situation resulting from Macdonald's bull-like personality prompted remedial action. A group of prominent golfing businessmen got together and invited a number of representatives of leading clubs—including Macdonald himself—to form an association to conduct the amateur and open championships. Thus the United States Golf Association was born and with it the first official amateur championship.

This time the result stood, which was pos-

The golfing manner when the century was young—
including a hot day in Vermont (top l.) and a hot drive
from pro Alex Pirie (above). Although long
skirts were lovely, they hampered women's swings.

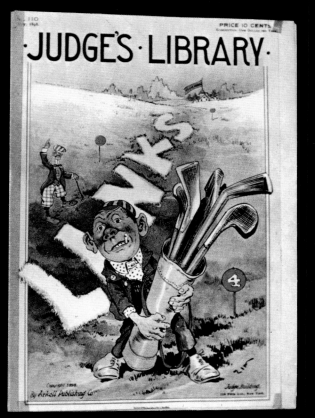

sibly less a reflection of the authority of the new body than of the fact that the winner was Macdonald. The man who had twice proved that he had the force of personality to upset the golfing applecart now turned his massive powers to the defense of the golfing establishment. With the maverick safely yoked, the path of progress was clear. As to the standard of American golf in these early years, some indication can be gleaned from Macdonald's figures of 89 and 100 in that first, abortive championship. In the first round, at least, he was sober enough and that was the leading score.

In the ten years between 1890 and 1900 American golf blossomed from one scrubby pasture course to more than a thousand. The standard of golf was of the novice variety for the most part, and if most of the courses, such as those of the Bendelow variety, were little more than good fields spoiled, there was one exception. The course built at Chicago at this time set a high standard and established a level of quality from which later architects were to take their soundings. It was designed by Charles Blair Macdonald.

For thirty years or so after the rise of the Apple-Tree Gang, the game spread through only one stratum of society. It was a rich man's sport and a snobbish one. New clubs were formed and immigrant Scottish professionals were engaged to teach the new game and supervise the construction of courses. The first municipal course was opened (in Boston) in 1890, and American technical ingenuity produced the rubber-core ball. But as far as the broad mass of the population was concerned, golf was a foreign fad for the nobs. On a competitive level, Walter Travis's victory in the British Amateur Championship in 1904 was a false dawn. Overseas players and foreign-born residents continued to monopolize the major competitions. Even the famous victory of the American amateur, Francis Ouimet, in

The genus Caddie was the butt of much satirical fun
in popular prints around 1900. In reality
the caddie worked too hard and for too little reward
to be able to appreciate the jokes.

beating the English champions Harry Vardon and Ted Ray in the U.S. Open of 1913, failed to capture public imagination. The newspapers made little of it, reflecting the general indifference to the game. Any impetus which might have been given to golf by Ouimet's triumph was stifled by the onset of World War I. For a time, America was to be preoccupied with more serious events.

With the armistice came a vast change. The Roaring Twenties produced a mood of national euphoria. America put up the shutters to the outside world, rolled back the carpet, and had a ball. This was the time when golf boomed. Many people see the game's expansion as a natural extension of the fun-loving atmosphere of jazz, flappers, and a national appetite for recreation. The real reason is possibly more prosaic. Rather than being swept in on a river of bootleg booze, golf owed its expansion to economics and the growth of the motor industry. People were making money and the cheap and reliable automobile was widely available. It was a period when sportsmen became national heroes and the golf professional in his turn benefited from the trend. American players dominated the championships, America dominated the game. Golf shed the last trap-

pings of Scottish influence and became a national game.

By 1931 there were two hundred and eighty-three flourishing public courses and golf was established as a sport for everyman. Tournament golf had progressed to purses of $10,000, and—although it was still a minority sport in terms of spectators—golf news was beginning to be accepted and looked for on the sports pages by the great newspaper-reading public.

The quality of the courses built to cater to the expanding game was a significant factor in the rise of American golf. The new school of golf architecture no longer looked to the links of Ayrshire and Fife for inspiration. Architects, adopting an analytical approach to the problem, produced designs suited to the terrain. They built fine, tightly bunkered courses which forced the golfer to plan his tactical approach and to execute shots of great accuracy. Of course, such requirements also obtained on the Scottish links, but there they were mainly imposed by the ever-present wind. The American architects built strategy into the topography of their courses.

As a result, the thirties and forties saw a subtle revolution in golfing technique. Harry Vardon

Dress fashions for golf reflected everyday clothing. Usually, the only special item for golf was a pair of walking boots with tackety studs hammered into the soles.

had popularized the conception of good style, but his golf was mainly a matter of improvisation; playing into a blasting forty-mile-per-hour wind, he used a swing quite different from that for a similar shot in still air. American players had a different set of problems. Most of the time wind was not a hazard. On the other hand, they had to meet a higher standard of accuracy.

A new breed of technicians—Ben Hogan, Byron Nelson, Sam Snead—sought basically to hit the ball just as Vardon did, but they achieved their aim with minor variations on the same repeating, grooved swing. Their example inspired a craze for analysis, technical instruction, and aids to the perfect swing. Hardly a part of the human anatomy escaped recognition as the "key" to good golf. Amateurs were awash in a flood of literature exhorting them to move their left thumbs a quarter of an inch around the shaft, or to concentrate on digging in the big toe of the right foot on impact. Much good it did them.

But for the masters, the standard of golf was raised to an unprecedented level of excellence. Seeing these Americans swing on visits to windswept St. Andrews, knowing Scots shook their heads and prophesied that the Yanks would be blown off the course. Two generations of American golfers have proved them wrong. Perhaps a whole winter of gales would ruin a grooved American swing, but on short visits American golfers do not have time to succumb to wind-cheating methods. Their style has stood the challenge year after year in the British Open and proved the efficiency of the American way of golf.

The triumphs of American professionals after World War II, not to mention the enthusiasm of a golfing president in the White House, encouraged another period of expansion.

At this time an ex-Coast Guardsman named Arnold Palmer asked Mark McCormack if he would manage his affairs as a professional golfer. McCormack, who had played on his college golf team and was just setting out on a law career, agreed. There was no formal contract, and at the outset McCormack limited himself to setting up exhibition matches. With Palmer freed of administrative details and able to concentrate singlemindedly on his game, his career, which had begun with high promise, quickly prospered to a degree which made him the most astonishing phenomenon in modern sport. Palmer's success had repercussions in every corner of the world. There is no profit in pursuing the chicken-and-egg question of whether McCormack made Palmer, or Palmer made McCormack. Their contributions were complementary.

In the early days of Palmer's career each victory, and every headline extolling the excitement his swashbuckling golf generated, gave McCormack another negotiating lever. He was soon in the driver's seat and dictating terms. Everybody wanted Palmer, and McCormack was calling the price. The squeals of anguish from the smoke-filled rooms reverberated across the land, and if McCormack won few friends in the process, he earned a grudging respect. As Palmer became a national figure, McCormack spread his activities beyond conventional golf contracts. He proved that the Palmer name could sell anything from dry cleaning to real estate. Palmer's commercial involvements grew into a million-dollar enterprise. Nobody doubted that McCormack was good for Palmer; but the question many people asked was whether McCormack was good for golf.

In the sense of performing altruistic acts, McCormack himself probably would not claim to have heaped benefits on the game. However, in the broader sense, no single man has done more for golf. Everyone whose living is dependent on golf has benefited from his influence. In 1941, the pro golf tour was worth less than $200,000 a year in prize money. During the time Palmer was the biggest attraction in golf the purse rose to $5 million. When McCormack negotiates for one of his clients—who have included Gary Player and Jack

The social status of golf is reflected in the opulence of the Glen Cove, New York, club, but by the twenties the broader appeal of the game was being celebrated, and propagated, in the songs of the day.

82

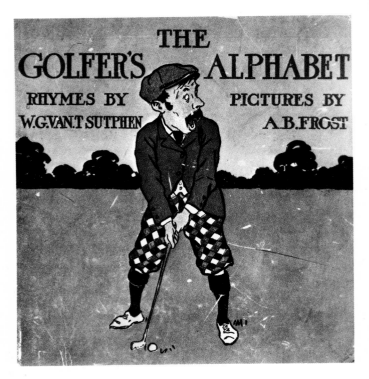

THE
GOLFER'S ALPHABET

RHYMES BY
W.G.VAN.T SUTPHEN

PICTURES BY
A.B.FROST

D is the Duffer, the Drive
    that he cuts,
And the Something he says when he
    misses short putts.

M is that Moment of
    agony keen
When it's one for the Match
    on the very last green.

R is the Rub that may lay
    us up dead,
Or leave us in sand buried
    over the head.

G is the Game we expected
to play,
But which didn't come off on
the tournament day.

J is the Jerk that would
drive in a pile,
But the ball, as you see,
wears a cynical
smile.

N is the Niblick, retriever
of blunders,
And now and again it accomplishes
wonders.

O is the Odd that we play
for the tin,—
Peculiar indeed that it
doesn't get in.

X is the X-pletive
sometimes employed.
For a golfer is human, and
easily annoyed.

Z is for Zero, the sign of
despair.
"Awa' wi' your gowf! we
will play it nae mair."

Nicklaus—he negotiates incidentally for every professional. The contracts he signs inevitably raise the rates for all. All professional golfers have been swept along in McCormack's slipstream to a new standard of living.

There have, of course, been many contributing factors to the growth of professional golf. Television has had enormous impact, both in popularizing the sport and in propagating it as the result of specially filmed competitions and general enlargement of purses. Golf was expanding, anyway, in the warm sun of the affluent society, and the pressures of inflation tended to push the prize funds upward. But the process was certainly accelerated by Palmer's golf and personality, and by his manager's acute exploitation of them.

If critics must still ask what McCormack

has done for golf, there are two major achievements for which he must be given a share of the credit. He was instrumental in reviving the flagging reputation of the British Open Championship by his policy of encouraging his players to attain international status. Today no championship in the world attracts a stronger field than the Open and by that token, at least, it is not only the oldest but the greatest of the Big Four grand-slam events. McCormack's part in the creation of the Piccadilly World Match Championship was even more direct. It was his baby, and at first was seen as something of a McCormack benefit. Over the years, however, it has grown in stature and now ranks highly in international esteem. Invitations to compete in the eight-man field are eagerly sought and the winner counts his success

Timeless drawings by A. B. Frost (preceding pages) and period knicknacks, including Bobby Jones statuette and McCoy golf recorder (opposite), found market among golfers—such as wealthy mandarins of the game (above).

Americans triumphed at Brookline in 1913.
Francis Ouimet (above), with caddie Eddie Lowery, on
his way to U. S. Open eclipse of Britain's
mighty Ted Ray (opposite, on left) and Harry Vardon.

high among his achievements.

The spread of golf has been accompanied by wide social repercussions. Although the game belongs to the masses as a major spectator sport and is played at every level of class and income—by ten million people in the U.S. alone—it has retained the aura of a gentlemanly activity.

In some ways golf's status has been elevated. The club professional, for instance, ranks in the community with the doctor and other professional men, whereas twenty years ago he was regarded on the level of a skilled artisan. The big-name tournament player walks with kings, and no one raises an eyebrow when he is invited to dine with the President. As for the young caddie who shows an aptitude for the game, he no longer aspires to an assistantship sweeping out the shop, but is induced to enter college on a generous scholarship. Golf remains a prestige game and the manufacturer who wants to stress the quality of his product uses a golfing association in his advertising. And it is undoubtedly true that golf does convey the image of style, good breeding, and a healthy out-of-doors feeling exuding the tang of pine needles and masculinity.

Alas the picture is illusory. The Madison Avenue idea that the golfer is a man for whom only the best is good enough and who, furthermore, makes it big with the dollies is sheer fiction (at least as far as his powers of discretion are concerned). In reality, once a man takes a golf club in hand he becomes a gullible idiot. For proof you have only to watch him on the course. The president of a large company, whose daily decisions affect the lives and well-being of thousands, escapes into a fantasy world in which he is a super-Nicklaus, judging by the shots he attempts. The cautious banker turns into a reckless gambler, going for the hundred-to-one chance of threading a three-iron through a two-foot gap in the woods. And after the game, still bereft of all their normal faculties, they read advertisements in the golfing press claiming that this glove will

More than anything else, the expanding car industry was responsible for the mushrooming popularity of golf, a popularity reflected in the decoration of articles of everyday use.

put yards on their drive or that a different brand of clubs will save them six shots a round.

It has been worked out that if all the claims in golfing advertisements were true, and a player equipped himself with the full range of magical new socks, gloves, clubs, balls, tees, shoes, and practice aids available to him, he would not only play to scratch within ten days, but the total promised extra yardage would have him driving the ball half a mile. And yet the captains of industry with speed slots and sweet spots dancing before their eyes, slide purposefully to the pro's shop and figuratively beg: "Please sell me the Brooklyn Bridge."

Despite this suspension of elementary common sense, the golf courses of the world have become extensions of business offices. Millions of dollars worth of business are transacted on golf courses every week. We can only hope that these golfing businessmen retain their professional acumen while conducting their *al fresco* discussions, even though on the golfing level they may have abandoned themselves to cuckooland. If golf adds a little oil to the cogs of domestic commerce, it supplies a positive gusher to the world of international business. It is the common ground on which the captains of industry can instantly find rapport.

In the bad old days, a visiting buyer might be feted around the night clubs and possibly introduced to the redhead in the front row of the chorus. Nowadays he is more likely to be taken out to the country club and partnered with the company's public-relations officer, who has been appointed to the job solely for his ability to get around in par or better after six martinis.

The value that corporations put on golf for purposes of good will was never more clearly demonstrated than in the Alcan tournament. The company allotted a vast budget for its promotion, which involved the co-sponsorship of qualifying tournaments in different parts of the world, culminating in a "Golfer of the Year" tournament with the richest first prize in golf.

The usual motives of commercial sponsorship were secondary in this case. The company was not particularly concerned about newspaper publicity or TV coverage, nor was the income from admissions an important factor in its budget calculations.

The format for the competition, involving total scores at the different qualifying events, was so complicated that it required lengthy calculations to keep track of a player's progress. The formula could have been simplified to make it readily understandable to the man in the street, and therefore more interesting, but here again the sponsors were noticeably unconcerned. Their prime motive was directly to influence business associates and potential customers. The outlay of millions of dollars was primarily for the benefit of a relatively few people, on one occasion no more than could be comfortably accommodated in the Gleneagles Hotel for the tournament at St. Andrews. Specially favored guests were allocated in the preliminary pro-am events. To an outsider one of the mysteries of these promotions was the arbitrary classification of guests according to their importance. For instance, a small customer would be given complimentary tickets to the tournament, another man would get, in addition, an invitation to the banquet, while the mighty moguls of aluminum would get a favored draw in the pro-am and a lavish trip to an overseas tournament.

You might expect human nature to react against such discrimination. A man would surely reason: "I may be only a small customer today but in a few years I could be the biggest aluminum consumer in the country. So where do these people get off handing me a gate ticket and a box lunch, while my rival is being put up in the best hotel in town and paired with Billy Casper in the pro-am?"

Most of us would surely bridle at such a slight and switch our business to a rival supplier. Not, apparently, so. During the five years of the Alcan tournaments, there was never a hint of acrimony on that

Golf becomes fashion conscious—or fashion becomes golf conscious. Either way, the Flapper Era was a swinging scene and the game was established in the American way of life.

92

JUNE 16, 1921 — Life — PRICE 15 CENTS

Golf
Number

The Wearing of the Green

5¢ a copy
10 Cents in Canada
July 21, 1923

Collier's
THE NATIONAL WEEKLY

Ena Crompton

In this issue:
They Call It Ruin by Richard Washburn Child

score. The sponsors were confident in their psychology that a man who had been omitted from the VIP list would react by striving harder than ever to win his way into favor by increasing his business the following year. We have seen that golf can cause rational people to behave in an irrational manner, but this probably was the first example of exploitation of golf's obsessive qualities in the cause of business.

More commonly, commerce uses golf for its associations. Alcohol and tobacco have to live down a continual assault from medicine and morality, and one of the ways this is achieved is by association with the healthy image of golf. The British Professional Golf cir-

cuit is mainly supported by cigarette and alcohol sponsors. American sponsorship has taken a different course. The vast dimensions of the nation have created a situation which makes it necessary for communities to advertise their importance. The resort town which shouts the loudest gets the tourist. If it is true that community spirit is stronger in America than anywhere else, it is also true that nowhere is community spirit so important to the economics of a city. As a result golf administrators all over the world look with envy and wonder at the American pro golf circuit, which is sustained by a gigantic voluntary effort. The message of a promotion like the Piccadilly World match-play championship is that

The making of a legend—Ben Hogan indicates
a round of 10 under par in Chicago in 1942 and eleven
years later, after winning the British Open,
receives a national hero's welcome on Broadway.

by association the great athletic heroes of golf endorse Piccadilly cigarettes.

The message of the Cleveland Open, on the other hand, is that Cleveland is a place with everything going for it, including Jack and Gary and Arnie. Cleveland's desire for publicity is helped by the fact that the only chance local golfers have to see the stars is to promote their own tournament. The country is so big that the golfing caravan can pass their way but once a year, and then only if the inducements are big enough. All these factors conspire to produce a goad which pricks the Clevelander in his two most sensitive areas: his billfold and his local pride. The result is a huge volunteer response. Armies of committees work from one year's end to the next to prove that anything Los Angeles can do Cleveland can do better. Los Angeles tries even harder, and so professional golf rides forward on a wave of local rivalry and volunteer effort.

Ed Carter, a professional administrator with responsibility for a number of tournaments, once costed a golf promotion on the assumption that prevailing rates would be paid for labor and equipment. It came to half a million dollars. Obviously, without voluntary labor from the business community, there could be no golf circuit at all.

Just look at the logistics of a tournament. First, a golf club must relinquish its course and premises for at least a week. Certain facilities—grandstands, tentage, and scoreboards—have to be provided. Players and officials need transport; up to two hundred cars and drivers must be made available. A complicated system of communications must be established to relay hole-by-hole scores to headquarters and back to the scoreboards. To accomplish all this, the tournament requires at least twenty skilled men to marshal the crowds at each hole, another hundred to operate the scoring and communications systems, a hundred or so to attend to such diverse activities as manning car parks, operating turnstiles, and organizing facilities within the club-

house. It is easy to see that even $500,000 would not go far if all the people had to be paid, especially for the many hours of preparatory work during the year before the event.

Imagine the reaction if anyone were so foolhardy as to walk into a British golf club, pick a member at random, and pose the question: "Would you like to serve on a tournament committee for a year, meeting for two hours every week, contribute the services of your office, equipment, and staff to the tournament, take a page advertisement in the program at an exorbitant rate, buy a uniform, and then take a week of your annual holiday to spend sitting in a tent relaying scores on a telephone?" The reply would be an explosion of indignant refusal, yet this is what happens all the time in America, and people fight for the privilege of volunteering.

With communities anxious to pour more and more cash and work into golf, the PGA's biggest problem is to select the richest plums. And all the while there is a rich fallout to charities. Unfortunately, there are times when some golfers lose sight of the source of their bounty. To the tournament player, of course, golf is a job and one week is much like the next. The point is that each week is the culmination of twelve months' hard work for the locals, and to them it is very special indeed. Hence, an unguarded comment about the quality of the course or a harsh word with a marshal may be a triviality to the golfer, but it is a blow to the victims. The PGA tries to indoctrinate its tournament recruits, but occasionally the lesson is forgotten. The golf circuit is a real-life example of a goose which lays golden eggs —a very good reason for taking great care not to ruffle its feathers.

If the volunteer worker is the backbone of American pro golf, the paying customer who buys his ticket at the gate is a very different proposition. Generally speaking, the golf spectator is less exuberant than the fan at the football or baseball match. Even so, he

Golf becomes a truly international sport. Gary Player and Neil Coles (top) in Piccadilly tournament, Wentworth, England, 1966, and Mark McCormack, man who guides the careers of golfing globe-trotters.

can get pretty involved; he has that great American birthright giving the man who has paid his dollar the right to express his opinion.

In Australia the sports fan does not admit that he goes to a match to support his team. He says he is a "barracker" for his team, meaning that he goes to jeer rather than cheer. The British like to consider themselves impartial, always excepting the oafish tradition of association football, and applaud skill no matter who displays it. That tradition is perhaps best seen at Wimbledon, where an outright winner is greeted with immediate applause. If the point is won by default, because of the opponent's misplay, there is a moment of silence in consideration for the victim before the ap-

lause begins for the winning of the point. Anyone who clapped immediately would be frowned out of the courts as a bounder. It is all very admirable in theory, but rather bloodless. It denies the essence of sport. Impartiality has no place in sport, which is cops-and-robbers in adult form. Certainly the enemy can be applauded, but this gesture should denote grudging admiration rather than lavish praise. Sport is partial. To become truly involved the spectator must associate with one side or one man and truly rejoice in his successes and grieve for his misfortunes.

This honest involvement is an American characteristic and explains the phenomenon of "Arnie's Army." Rooting for Palmer naturally involves seeing

Golf develops into a major spectator sport. Arnold Palmer sinks winning putt for 1964 Masters and (above) shares hero-worshipping with the man who was to topple him from the golfing pinnacle, Jack Nicklaus.

all other golfers as enemies, and if this explains the booing of Jack Nicklaus in the early days of his career, it does not necessarily excuse it. Eventually, the PGA took some of the heat out of golf watching by forbidding the carrying of banners on the course. Even so, the American golf watcher remains the loudest cheerer and the most fervent groaner in the world. In Britain it is possible with a little practice to interpret the course of a golf match by the noise of the gallery. The quality of the applause for a 20-foot putt to save a half is quite different from the reaction to a winning 20-footer. And if the putts miss (in silence, naturally), there are different reactions again for the tap-ins. In America, cheer interpretation is much more difficult. An explosion of glee on the other side of a hill may mean that Don January has holed out from a bunker, or simply that Palmer has made a joke on the tee. There was a time when an agonized groan could mean that Palmer had missed a putt or that Nicklaus had holed one.

At least, the reactions are genuine. When the late Tony Lema was engaged to play an exhibition round in Copenhagen, the organizers were so concerned to make him feel properly appreciated that they hired a large crowd of bemused spectators at $15 a head.

There was no shortage of curious spectators for Walter Hagen's exhibition match in Palestine (as it was then), but his opening drive, one of the best he had ever hit, was greeted by silence. His opponent hit a very poor effort which hopped feebly forward and received tumultuous applause. The explanation was that the spectators, completely unaccustomed to golf and having no idea what was supposed to happen, did not see Hagen's ball depart and having no clue where it had gone did not know if his shot was good or bad.

Golf is one of the few games where the fan has to follow the action on foot, and the logistics of moving several thousand people around a four-mile course are complex. There are two principal methods of handling a golf crowd. For bigger events the usual practice is to fence off the fairways and permit a free-for-all behind the ropes. The other method, and a vastly superior one where the circumstances permit, is to let galleries follow the golfers up the fairways under the supervision of marshals and stewards.

In both cases the fan will get more pleasure from his watching if he spends a moment or two in preliminary preparation. If the fairways are fenced and the crowds are dense, the best plan is to use the leapfrog technique. You take up your position behind a tee to give yourself the best possible view of the drives. After the players have hit their tee shots you resolutely ignore all temptations to see the second shots and march purposefully to the green and take up station directly behind the flag. In this way you have avoided the scramble of the herd and are in prime position to watch the putting. Once the players have holed out you allow the mob to dash to the next tee while you walk in dignified comfort to the place on the ropes where you judge the tee shots will finish. By this method you get a good view of every other shot, your progress unimpeded and your temper tranquil.

Compare that experience with the sweaty frustration of joining the stampede and trying your tiptoe best to watch every stroke. Watching golf can be more tiring than playing the game because of the infighting and standing about, shifting your weight from foot to foot. A brisk walk is positively refreshing in comparison to the scramble among the infantry of Arnie's Army, and the deplorable slowness of modern professional golf makes it preferable at times to follow one match for a hole and then leapfrog to the match in front. By this method you can get a sight of twenty-seven players by the time you reach the turn and pause for your well-earned beer. At that point you can decide whether to continue moving up through the field, or whether to wait and pick up one of the threesomes you have already seen.

Another variation is more suited to those

101

Vast resources of cash and equipment—
including effects mike and cherry-picker camera
hoist seen here—are deployed
to bring golf to the television screen.

enlightened fans who hold the opinion that life has no more tedious sight to offer than a pro golfer spending two minutes missing a 6-foot putt. After all, if a man has a one-iron shot over a ravine there is an infinite variety of possibilities as to the outcome. With that putt there are only two results—hit or miss—and the reaction of the crowd should indicate what happened. Confirmation, if needed, can usually be obtained by one of those eager beavers who run between shots in order to get into position for every moment of action. These flying advance scouts from the main body of troops are usually accurate witnesses to a simple question such as, "Did Casper hole that putt?" However, be warned never to trust any on-course intelligence reports of a more advanced nature. If the scout adds that Casper is now four under and needs only to par the last two holes for victory, treat the information with suspicion. It is nearly always wrong. You cannot guarantee that the scout is mistaken, of course, so the best method is to regard him as you would a clock which has just struck thirteen or the man who announced, "Every statement I make is a lie." Assume that this present statement is incorrect until it is confirmed (and, whisper it softly, there are times when a scoreboard on the course is not much more reliable than the gallery grapevine).

If you are at a tournament where you are privileged to walk on the fairways, certain adjustments can be made in the leapfrog method. The advantage now is that you have the privilege of inspecting the lie of the ball. Golf watching immediately takes on a new dimension. No matter how well prepared a golf course may be, every player will get a bad (or difficult) lie on the fairway on an average of once in three shots. Having seen his lie, you are in a much better position to appreciate his shot. Furthermore, having inspected the lie of the ball, you also have had the opportunity to visualize the shot the player must face, and this is very different from the problem you

Cameramen and commentators are positioned to relay action on the small screen. Golf is seen on even smaller screens by spectators jostling for vantage points with their periscopes.

have perceived from behind the ropes.

(Try this experiment the next time you play golf. When you come to a place where you have a good broadside view of a distant fairway, pause and watch the golfers playing their shots. Imagine what club you would select for the approach shot you are watching in the distance. To you, from your side view, it looks an even seven-iron. File away that judgment in your mind and bring it out when you reach that same fairway. What looked like an easy seven has suddenly become a full three-iron shot, preferably with a shade of draw to hold it up against the slope of the green. Golf is an easy game from outside the ropes.)

There is, in addition, one specific golfing bonus from allowing spectators to follow on the fairways. When the crowd is behind ropes or fences it must of necessity walk through the rough. That is, it starts off as rough. Very quickly, however, the rough is trampled flat and the player who sprays his drives is not penalized. At times some players take advantage of the crowd's depredations and aim deliberately to areas which would normally be high rough, knowing that they are sure of a playable lie. Nowadays it is increasingly rare to allow galleries onto the fairways, owing to the vast increase in crowds, the requirements of TV cameras to get unrestricted shots of the play, and the well-publicized (though not always disinterested) criticism of players. It is a pity, because for the true golf fan fairway watching is the only way to see the game. Unfortunately, whenever crowds are allowed onto fairways, there are always a few people who disrupt the system, either through bad manners or ignorance or sheer enthusiasm. It is here that effective marshaling is vital and all too often it fails.

Crowd control is a tricky business but doing it well is mostly a matter of good manners and common sense. The first requirement is to win the confidence of the mob. The worst mistake any marshal can make, and unfortunately it is the commonest, is to create a situation in which he, representing authority, commands obedience to arbitrary instructions. You, sir, are a reasonable man and as cooperative as anyone, but if a red-faced marshal yells at you, "Get back on the left, you people," at the same time thrusting a bamboo staff across your stomach, your reaction, having paid your hard-earned dollar to watch the golf, is to snap the bamboo across your knee and edge farther forward. We understand, sir, and forgive you. We applaud you for your spirit and sturdy independence. We all move farther forward. And we find ourselves in a situation where Arnold Palmer hands us his clubs and says, "You play my shot. You're standing closer to the ball." So we all laugh sheepishly and push back a yard or so.

The trouble is that the marshal tends to see the crowd as an entity, as a flock of sheep to be manipulated. But although we do display a herd instinct in some ways, we are all individuals and determined to maneuver into the best positions. If the marshal adopts a hectoring attitude, he becomes our enemy and we naturally feel free to outwit him the best we can. However, there is a way, and that is for the marshal to win us over. Instead of yelling, "Hold it right there," he can simply suggest, "If we make a circle here, we all can see." Immediately we are all on the same side and, with a certain amount of common sense, an orderly and disciplined gallery can watch in comfort and good humor. In short, golf watchers can be led but not driven. It is a lesson few marshals ever master completely.

This problem of crowd control is perhaps more acute in Britain and mainland Europe than in America, but that is no reason why golf administrators should ignore it. If more attention were paid to crowd-managing techniques perhaps more tournaments could permit the galleries onto the fairways, and that would benefit everyone. But the attitude has been fostered that the golf spectator is a necessary evil, to be tolerated as long as he behaves himself, on the grounds that first priority must be given to the golf and the golfers. Quite right. Nobody would suggest that spectator facilities should be developed to the detriment of the golf; but that is no reason why the paying fan should not receive every possible consideration.

Today we hear more and more frequently of golf fans who say they prefer to watch a tournament on television. TV has done extremely well in popularizing golf and educating the public about it. For instant analysis of the golf swing, the techniques developed by TV—stop-action, slow-motion replay, and split-screen shots showing a golfer making his stroke from two angles simultaneously—are superb. Backed by a knowing commentator, TV golf is a valuable tutor.

At the same time it must be said that TV golf is a vastly inferior substitute for the real thing. At the present state of technical development, with static cameras covering a few selected holes, TV shows part of the game and gives only a sketchy impression of that part.

Looking sideways at a distant fairway, shots may seem easy. Very seldom can the camera convey the problem from the golfer's standpoint. And the nature of the game forces the TV producer to focus on the longueurs of the putting ritual. Here again the game is diminished because the camera's-eye view flattens the contours of the green and makes every putt appear level. The worst by-product of this situation is that the viewer sitting at home is indoctrinated with the fallacious idea that in order to miss a 4-foot putt it is necessary first to remove one's glove, inspect the putt from every point in the compass, pick up imaginary grains of sand from the line, and indulge in a lengthy practice session away from the ball in order, presumably, to invent a method of striking it. In fact, you can miss that putt (or indeed hole it) just as certainly if you step straight up to it and give the ball a tap. All over in a few seconds. Honestly, it's true. You can.

To be fair—as if that were much of a virtue in this context—much of the tedium on the green is caused by the knowledge that the time has to be filled somehow. If the players putted out briskly they would only have an even longer wait on the next tee while the players in front moved out of range. (There are also those who believe that there is a law of diminishing returns on the green and that there comes a point, after a certain period of reconnaissance, when the longer a golfer delays the moment of striking the less likely he is to hole out.)

The administrators of golf are concerned with speeding up tournament golf because of the bad example to club players. At a time when the building of new courses is lagging far behind public demand, it is unfortunate that existing courses are clogged by four-balls taking up to six hours for eighteen holes. There was a time when a day's golf meant a full round in the morning, another eighteen after lunch, and then nine holes of fun golf, using perhaps one club only, in the evening. Imagine trying to do that on a modern course. The pros do a good job for the club game, but inadvertently by their example they are also spoiling it. As things are going, the need for some rule on time may become acute. All manner of suggestions have been made, and possibly the chess players' practice of "starting the opponent's clock" may suggest a helpful convention, if not a firm rule, which golf clubs could adopt. For example, once a man has reached his ball, he would be required to play the shot within, say, 30 seconds, and on the green, having replaced his ball after marking, he would be permitted perhaps no more than 15 seconds.

Such drastic measures could be avoided, however, if the members of the golfing public stopped thinking of themselves as tournament-playing pros and let themselves be drawn—by the simple pleasures of the game—back into the righteous path of speedy golf as the Scots gave it to us.

4 · a universal passion

For a Victorian gentleman, the highest estate to which any human being could aspire was that of the Victorian gentleman. In the heyday of British imperialism, therefore, when God was a middle-class Englishman, it was a Christian duty to bring enlightenment to the world and to convert everyone into replicas of Victorian gentlemen. Civilization meant, simply, the English way of life. It naturally followed that those sons of the shires took with them to the far posts of Empire not only their commercial acumen and missionary zeal, but also the household gods of their society. The holds of the P. & O. liners were packed with tennis racquets, cricket bats, golf clubs, port decanters, dinner jackets, and hunting kits. And on arrival in some tropical fever swamp, the Englishman's first concern was to arrange his surroundings so that he might, with a little imagination and a lot of gin, believe himself never to have left Surrey. In short order he built a club, drained enough swamp to lay out tennis courts, cricket pitch, or golf course, and the wives held musical evenings every Wednesday. There were many corners of foreign jungles which were forever Weybridge.

As social changes rearranged the quality of life back in England, these colonial outposts remained faithful to a vision of a vanished England—snobbish and pathetic parodies of a bygone age. But they made their imprint on the overseas countries, particularly in the field of our special concern.

You may think that these golf courses were built for the wrong reasons and for the wrong people. But in time, as intended, the indigenous populations did become close copies of Englishmen in their adoption of these weird pursuits. And very often the pupils became more enthusiastic and more skillful than the masters. In India, especially, the ball boys and caddies who were recruited to service the Anglo-Saxon games progressed to become professionals. They did not have to reach very high standards to shine by comparison with the sahibs. In the English code it is bad form to practice a game; it is only permissible to excel at games by virtue of a natural gift.

Golf clubs were established in India, the Far East, Australia, Canada, and Europe long before the end of the nineteenth century, and very strange courses they were, compared to the Scottish seaside courses on which they were supposedly modeled.

The other force which motivated the building of golf courses all over the world was the nature of the game itself. Golf has often been likened to an infection which gets into the bloodstream and cannot be eradicated. What is more, as we have seen, golf addiction can produce hallucinations, irrational behavior, and an insatiable craving. Whatever you like to call it, the obsessional nature of golf has manifested itself in some strange places.

In appearance, the oddest courses born of this addiction are those which have been built in deserts. Golf requires water, either natural rain or piped, to produce its full glory. The golfer relishes greenness. Phrases such as "lush turf" and "velvet greens" have an emotive force synonymous with excellence. No wonder many golfers believe that Ireland offers the finest golf courses in the world. Certainly they are the greenest, which is hardly surprising in a country where housewives habitually peep out of their cottage windows and observe that it is a beautiful day for hanging the washing out to rinse.

Whereas rain in Ireland is so commonplace that it is not even mentioned (a steady drizzle is greeted as "a nice soft day"), in some places it is so rare that for practical purposes it does not happen at all. The idea of pouring this precious commodity onto the ground to encourage grass to grow is so farfetched as to be out of the question. A favorite cartoon in the Middle East shows a prospector sinking a trial bore and replying to the inquiry, "Any luck?" with, "No, I keep on striking oil."

Preceding pages: St. Andrews, spiritual home of "the Anticient and healthfull Exercise of the Golf" and today capital of an empire embracing some fifty-five golfing nations.

Desert golf courses are literally "watered" with oil; instead of greens they have "browns," areas of leveled sand compacted with crude oil. At least one of the major professional tournaments on the African circuit is played on a course with browns, and there are many golf courses which cannot boast a single blade of grass. Hell, we tell ourselves, that is just not golf. But this is a highly prejudiced reaction. Basically, golf is a cross-country game ending with putting into a small hole, and grass as such is not necessary in any way to the golfer's progress. The club makes contact with the ball, which thereupon departs. Subsequently the club may gouge a divot of bleeding turf, but that of itself is of no consequence. The effect is exactly the same if, instead of a grassy divot, the club plows up a handful of dry grit.

Indeed, playing off hard-packed sand may improve the game because it requires a more accurate technique. Christy O'Connor, the great Irish golfer, is generally acknowledged to be one of the finest strikers of a golf ball of his generation and a genuinely natural player. While it may be true that he never had a formal lesson, it is absurd to suggest that he was born with his swing. He learned his golf by trial and error, and the place where he learned was on the hard-packed sands of Dublin Bay. He learned to strike the ball accurately because that was the only way that worked. A slight mis-hit off grass may produce a satisfactory result as the club slices through the soft turf. The same shot from sand goes nowhere.

In the same way, the professionals of the Far East who play on hard, bare courses much of the time, have evolved a short-game technique which is uncanny in its accuracy. Where the western professional squeezes the ball into the turf with his wedge, the easterner flicks the ball cleanly off the unyielding surface. All in all, then, that part of golf which we call "through the green" can be every bit as satisfying when it is played "through the brown."

But what of putting? Surely you cannot putt as well on an oily patch of sand as you can on a well-tended grass surface? In fact, once you have adjusted to the difference in pace, putting on browns is considerably more consistent. Any irregularity is obvious to the naked eye. No matter how closely the golfer studies his line on a green he cannot see the worm casts and spike marks below the surface of the grass. What is more, on a green there is often the problem of nap, or grain, and he must try to guess how his ball will be deflected by the direction in which the grass lies. The usual practice after putting on browns is to drag a doormat over the surface to smooth the irregularities you have created. So everyone gets a pristine surface for his putt.

In one major respect, however, the "brown" golfers are truly underprivileged. If we hold the view that half of golf is the aesthetic experience—being surrounded by beautiful countryside—then the desert version is only half a game.

Not so mountain golf. Mountains offer an unusual and spectacular terrain. While the purist may scoff, mountain golf is an exhilarating experience every golfer should sample if he can. For a start, there is Capilano, which perches dramatically on a mountain in the Canadian Rockies overlooking Vancouver. Although its elevation frequently provides the eerie experience of playing above the clouds, it does not qualify as a true mountain course since it is built on a gentle escarpment. The fairways slope rather than plunge, and the player who walks the course does not risk a coronary. In the same way, Crans-sur-Sierre is set so high in the Swiss Alps that the ball flies prodigious distances in the rarefied air. (When the Swiss Open is played here the pros get up at a par-5 hole with a drive and a nine-iron.) Again, the slopes underfoot are gentle. Both courses are worthy of a pilgrimage, as is Banff for the majesty of its surroundings; but for real mountain golf we must go to a course like Semmering,

in Austria. This is set in picture-postcard country of isolated farmsteads high among the peaks, with cowbells tinkling in the Alpine meadows. Here the golfer must have calf muscles like steel hawsers. A wayward drive can literally travel a mile, bouncing down, down, down into the misty valleys. You drive blind over brows, slice violently in an attempt to hold up your ball on a wicked sideslope, and take extravagant care not to overshoot a green which may be sited on the brink of a ravine. It is trick-shot golf and one of the tricks the visitor soon discovers is that it is advisable to use the clouds as points of aim. Nowhere is this more necessary than on one short hole which is a sheer drop.

You inch nervously to the front of the tee, fighting vertigo, and there, directly below, is a tiny shelf of a green set into the side of the plunging mountain. Miss that green and the ball will bounce down into oblivion. It seems that you could spit onto that green, but that diagnosis is not too helpful since it is impossible to translate into a golf shot. Should you tee up the ball and simply flip it over the end of the tee with a putter and let gravity take care of the rest? In fact, surprising as it may seem, it is all too easy to be short here. No matter how unlikely it may appear looking down from above, the ball will stop and lodge on that fierce gradient. The trick is to pick a convenient cloud in line with

Variations on the theme of golf—oceanic at Castle Harbour, Bermuda (above); mountainous, at Crans-sur-Sierre, Switzerland (opposite, top); pastoral at Acquasanta, Rome.

the flag, take a firm command of your nervous qualms and hit a full wedge out over the precipice. The ball, plummeting vertically, splats into the turf and buries itself up to the waist for one of the most unusual and satisfying experiences golf has to offer.

Any writer who attempts to describe American golf courses simply sets himself up as an Aunt Sally to be knocked down. Even the blandest generalization is overwhelmed by the weight of the exceptions which prove it false. Many visitors remark that wind is not as important a factor in the U.S. as elsewhere. True enough, as far as it goes. But formulate that observation as a dogmatic statement—"generally speaking, American golf is played in still air or gentle breezes"—and the writer leaves himself wide open to a flurry of counterpunches. Golfers on both seaboards snarl at such ignorance, and the sand-blasted enthusiasts of West Texas, glaring from behind the motorcyclist's goggles they are obliged to wear, drawl, "The wind in Texas is the strongest in the world." From the wreckage of the argument we are left with the conclusion that in some places the wind is strong some of the time and in others it isn't some of the time. The thought is not worth expressing.

What then of the widely held view that American greens are watered to a spongy consistency which turns the game into outdoor darts, with every approach shot plugging where it lands? Again, the half-truth is matched by the half-lie. On the evidence of the great championships, you could as well claim that American greens are the fastest in the world.

The fact is that there is no such thing as the American golf course. In the North, courses are closed for the winter and in the South some are closed for the summer. On a continent which spreads from the Arctic to the tropics, every type of course is to be found. The American course is as diverse as the American golfer.

Having established that the American golf course does not exist, and having therefore disarmed criticism in advance, it is perhaps possible to isolate one common type of course and identify some of its typical features. This is what we might call the middle course—the middle-class, middle-income, country-club course found through the central states—which represents a sizable proportion of American golf. The visiting Briton is immediately struck by certain basic differences between the American golf course and the British, the chief one being that American golfers value comfort and luxury and are willing and able to pay for it. Many British club members have incomes which do not amount to $2,000 a year, and they fight to keep the cost of golf as low as possible. The annual dues at some of the "best" clubs around London, where demand so far exceeds supply that most clubs have two-year waiting lists for membership, averages about $100. Needless to say, very few British clubs offer anything like the clubhouse accommodations and facilities found in American counterparts. The British tradition is for a functional, if not downright spartan, clubhouse—a place to change, have a drink after the game, and perhaps enjoy a light meal. The clubhouse exists to service the needs of golf. Social activities at these clubs are limited. When a British golfer finds a companionable party raising the rafters in his club, he knows a visiting golf society is playing that day. Indeed, there is a breed of golfer—and quite numerous he is—known as a "car-park member," who rarely enters the club at all.

The American club, by contrast, is much more of a family affair. The club probably will offer tennis, swimming, and indoor game rooms as well as golf. The members will see their club as a community center. Private rooms will be hired for family celebrations and wedding receptions, and it is by no means exceptional for members to be required to spend $2,000 a year in the club. It also is not unusual for members to assume their share of the club's indebtedness by purchasing debentures when they join, which gives

With protective goggles and a touch of
fanaticism golf flourishes in the most inhospitable
surroundings—even among the sand dunes of
the Namid Desert of South-West Africa at Walvis Bay.

112

everyone a real sense of participation in, and obligation to, the club.

A Briton entering an American country club, providing he survives the tidal wave of hospitality, will notice certain differences about the course. Mainly they will be points of emphasis. Fairways on the whole will be wider, and the rough, such as it is, seems short both in length and in menace. (He may revise the latter view when he discovers the tough texture of the grass.) He may also form the opinion that the architect has rather overdone the number of trees, sand bunkers, water hazards, and the size of the greens. The effect is that these courses encourage the golfer to swing without undue inhibition in the knowledge that the scale of punishments for a wild stroke is a fair one. The golf course will give him what he deserves. In Britain and Ireland, as a broad generalization, the golfer tends to be inhibited by the course with its narrower fairways, penal rough, and daunting feeling that quite a good shot may be punished severely. If anyone cares to draw conclusions as to whether conditioning by these two types of courses accounts for the performance gap between the leading professionals of the two countries, he is at liberty to do so. Most American pros approach the game more aggressively than most Britons.

It might be inferred from all this that at

championship level the British courses are tougher tests of golf, and this conclusion might be justified if championships were played on courses in their everyday condition. This, as we all know, is not the case. A year of preparation goes into transforming the landscape for the U.S. Open. In country-club trim, a course like Merion is, with the exception of the last four holes, not unduly difficult compared with, say, Carnoustie. But by the time fertilizer by the ton has been lavished upon it to encourage the rough, and the rough has been allowed to grow into the fairways, it is a totally different proposition, especially with the greens dehydrated to the USGA's sadistic specifications.

At the highest championship level there is little difference between the standards of the shot-making test set by the examiners whether the event is played at Pinehurst, St. Andrews, or Royal Melbourne. The critical factor is the great unknown, the weather. Since the R. and A. insists on holding the British Open on seaside courses, it is practically guaranteed that at some stage in their championship the weather will make a decisive and generally unpleasant intervention.

Golf on marvelous courses in spectacular settings is now tourist bait the world over. Spain, Portugal, and—somewhat belatedly—Italy are encouraging golf and golfers. France was slow to appreciate the drawing power of golf, possibly because she is so rich in tourist attractions of other kinds. On the other hand, Yugoslavia has embarked on an ambitious program to cultivate golf—for itself as well as for its visitors. The Yugoslavs are undertaking to build fifty courses and are adopting golf as a native game.

Island paradises—from Bermuda to the Caribbean, and from Hawaii to Fiji in the Pacific—are attracting tourists with a new breed of golf course. Once a bulldozer has cleared the fairways and the surface of coral rock has been prepared, the seedling grasses need only a plentiful supply of water to create what is virtually an instant course. For the visitor these

"The finest meeting of land and sea in the world"—the Monterey Peninsula's golfing treasury has no equal to Pebble Beach, whose 9th hole often effects a meeting between golf ball and sea.

lush playgrounds offer a novel experience. If he misses a fairway he must reconcile himself to a lost ball, because any attempt to penetrate the thick jungle of undergrowth is doomed. He will seldom recover his ball and may do himself some injury in the search. On some of the beautiful Bahamian courses a local rule permits a player to drop another ball on the fairway opposite the point where his shot entered the tangle of vegetation, under penalty of a stroke, of course, and the professional's shop does a healthy trade in packs of cheap pick-ups.

Just as English colonists introduced golf to the British Empire, so in a similar situation Americans introduced golf to Japan. The forces of occupation after World War II built courses for the troops' recreation and soon the Japanese took to the new game, just as they adopted baseball. If we in the West consider ourselves to be slightly unhinged in our enthusiasm for golf, it is nothing to the reaction of the Japanese. They took up the game with almost religious fervor which quickly proved an embarrassment to this small, highly populated, industrial country. With such intense competition for land from agriculture, housing, and industry, golf was possibly not the most appropriate game for a new national mania. A chess boom they could have handled, or even an epidemic of pole squatting. However, golf was not to be denied, never mind if it did need some two hundred acres of precious land for every course.

Thanks to an economic miracle there was no shortage of wealthy patrons and enough courses have been built to accommodate some four million golfers. Unfortunately that still leaves another four million golfers (some authorities claim six million) with nowhere to play. You might think that in such a situation the hordes of frustrated would-be golfers would become discouraged, sell their clubs, and take up another hobby. Any such conjecture misjudges the appeal

Clubhouse styles vary from that of Shinnecock Hills, where the American tradition of spacious luxury was established, to Byzantine architecture of the Medinah Country Club in Illinois (above).

Gracious golf in the South: The incomparable
Augusta National club with two water-threatened
short holes, the 16th (above) and the
12th, and a tastefully understated Georgian clubhouse.

of golf and the nature of the Japanese. They insist on playing. The solution to this intractable problem was to build driving ranges, if such an outcome can be dignified by the word solution.

There are no fewer than three hundred ranges in Tokyo alone, all of them thriving. They vary in size and scope from small halls with a net at the far wall and mats for half a dozen players, to a building the size of a department store with three tiers of driving bays, where the scale of charges varies as in a theater, with ground floor stalls most expensive. All the ranges prosper. Day or night they are crowded by enthusiastic golfers. Office workers devote their lunch breaks to hitting buckets of balls. Many of these embryo golfers will never have the opportunity to play on a real course; they will never know the satisfaction of hitting a golf ball off crisp green turf, of exploding from sand, or rolling a putt across a velvet lawn. Heather,

bracken, gorse, and tufted grass will never cleave to their nine-irons and no tree will stymie their approaches. Not knowing golf's agonies they cannot really know its joys, but they do not seem to mind.

Even scoring, which we luckier golfers hold to be central to the game, does not concern them. One would imagine, with such an involvement in range golf, that a new game would evolve with standardized targets and a regulated scoring system, a variety of golfing archery, if you like. But no. For the Japanese range golfers the hitting of a ball seems a sufficient end in itself.

For those Japanese who can afford to join a club or patronize a municipal course, the game is superficially far removed from the Scottish prototype. It offers nothing similar to the spartan granite clubhouses of Fife with their wasteland courses of bleak dunes and arthritic trees stunted and bowed by

Opposite: Sunningdale, England (top), and Ireland's Portmarnock—where wind gauge in the bar helps members decide whether it would be more prudent to remain indoors. Above: Rugged country of Long Reef, Sydney, Australia.

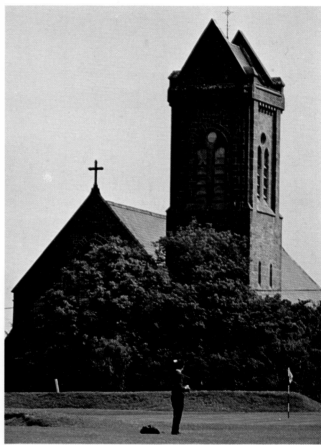

*Majestic and magical golf of Ireland: Royal
Portrush in the north (opposite) and, with four-legged
mower-fertilizers, Lucan, near Dublin
(top). Above: Castletroy, Limerick, with adjacent confessional.*

Golf-mad Japan—with multi-tier driving ranges, women caddies, bilingual markers, and parasols all contributing to the distinction of the modern tee ritual.

the prevailing gales. Where a Scottish architect naturally tends to produce a prison-cell-block of a clubhouse and the American tends to the gin-palace school of design, the Japanese draftman's plans come out as temples. The visiting westerner is made to feel that he should remove his shoes and speak in a respectful whisper in a Japanese clubhouse. The idea that a building should be merely functional is as repugnant to a good Japanese architect as that it should be tarted up with gewgaws and gimmickry.

That tradition extends to the course itself. There are many American courses where trees and shrubs are planted with extreme care to achieve continuity of flowering and aesthetic effect, but the Japanese see their golf courses as gardens, Japanese gardens, of course, with trim beds of chrysanthemums bordering the tees, trees painstakingly cultured into satisfying shapes, and crystal-clear water hazards floored with hand-picked stones and stocked with ornamental fish and flowering plants. It is positive pleasure to slice into a Japanese pond.

All this requires an army of maintenance staff, and when labor charges are added to the prohibitive cost of the land, Japanese golf becomes an extremely expensive occupation. A man must be rich, or have a generous expense account, to consider joining a club and in some cases he must satisfy stringent social requirements. At some clubs a potential member has to be entered at birth, as at an exclusive school, or inherit his membership—and his proportionate share of the debentures. He will have to pay large annual dues plus, in some cases, additional green fees for every round he plays.

To the Japanese it is worth every yen, especially if he is in business. In the world of commerce, nothing carries more status points than membership in a golf club. It stamps the Japanese businessman as a fellow of substance and, at the same time, helps him professionally by putting him on a man-to-

124

*Morocco, where royal patronage
(that's the king's private entrance to the course
from his palace) has started a golf boom
which extends even to the bazaars of Marrakesh.*

man footing with the leaders of industry. If martinis at the 19th are the lubricant of American industry, clubhouse green tea serves the same purpose in Japan.

The exotic trimmings of Japanese clubhouses and courses are only a veneer. When the Japanese golfer takes club in hand he may be attended by a teen-age girl caddie, whose burden is increased by a bag of sand and grass seed to dress the scars on the precious turf, but inside he is the same as any other golfer. A thousand years of unique culture may have produced a race with little in common with western man, but down among those primitive instincts and emotions that are stirred by golf all men are equal in their struggle to attain a goal which is so clearly within their grasp and yet remains elusive. Golf unites all men in universal frustration.

One other custom separates the Japanese golfer and that is the tradition of gambling. The high rollers are almost unknown in Japan, where no matter how wealthy a man may be his stake on that Sunday morning four-ball will be purely notional. At one wealthy club the tradition has grown of playing for a bar of chocolate, and some token on this order is the common currency. Like his compatriot on the driving range, the Japanese player holds golf to be a sufficient end in itself and winning its own reward.

Golf mania in Japan is fired by extensive coverage in the papers. Hardly a day passes when golf is not presented in some form on television. The professionals have a strong tournament program and the best Japanese pros can hold their own against anyone. There is no question that the Japanese are second only to the Americans in the ranks of international golf.

The Japanese experience is repeated in a somewhat modified version in Taiwan. Here again the American allies popularized golf and the local population took up the game in some numbers. Possibly the clearest indication of the growing strength of Chinese golfers was seen in the British Open Championship at Royal Birkdale in 1971, when Lu Liang Huan chased Lee Trevino all the way home and came within two strokes of creating the biggest upset in modern golf.

On the continent of Africa golf is mainly the preserve of the white population in the old colonial tradition, although some notable exceptions are beginning to emerge with the changing political situation of the newly independent nations. The game came to Egypt as a legacy of British rule, but has long since been absorbed into the national life, albeit as a rich man's game. In Morocco the enthusiasm of the golfing King Hassan has given enormous stimulus to the game. The first major international golf event in Morocco was interrupted by a bloody battle when revolutionaries invaded the links and tried to overthrow the loyal government. The king survived the attempted coup and so, in consequence, did the game of golf.

Africa maintains two professional golf circuits, one in the Republic of South Africa and the other among the newly independent nations to the north. In South Africa golf is strictly segregated—like all other aspects of life. Blacks and Cape Coloreds who have an opportunity to play the game at all are restricted to their own courses which are very inferior affairs, indeed.

One way or another, golf has spread to almost every corner of the world, from tropical deserts to the glaciers of Iceland. But perhaps the strangest manifestation of the game's resilience in a hostile environment occurred in 1943, in the middle of World War II. In Britain at that time golf balls were unobtainable, and many courses were taken over to grow food. A few fortunates continued to play intermittently, with a pathological concern not to lose a precious, scarred veteran of a ball such as today would be discarded from anyone's practice bag. Special local rules were approved to permit players to replace balls moved by enemy action (many courses still retain bomb craters as legacies of this period), or to lift and drop clear of unexploded bombs.

If you feel that golf could hardly survive even worse conditions than this you would be wrong. There was one course where the penalty for being out of bounds was not the loss of a stroke or the loss of a ball but quite possibly the loss of life! Pat Ward-Thomas, who later became golf correspondent of *The Manchester Guardian,* was shot down on a bombing raid over Germany and imprisoned in Stalag Luft 3, the main camp for air-crew officers. Soon after his arrival, a hickory-shafted ladies' mashie turned up in the camp and its discovery caused great excitement. How such an unlikely implement came to be in a POW camp in the middle of the forest of Sagan nobody knew. Or cared. Immediately the history of the golf ball was reenacted in miniature. The prisoners' first ball was made by winding string around a wooden core and covering it with cloth. Then someone found some shreds of rubber and, just like Sandy Herd with the coming of the Haskell rubber-core ball, he spread-eagled the field with his jerry-built missile. Some tried to remain faithful to their string gutties, but progress would not be denied. The rubber-bound ball, covered with medical sticking plaster, had come to stay. The technique was further refined by cutting up rubber-soled shoes and producing leather-covered balls which conformed exactly to the specifications of the Royal and Ancient Golf Club: 1.62 inches in diameter and 1.62 ounces in weight.

As the golf craze grew, the prisoners turned their attention to clubmaking. Shafts were whittled by penknife and heads cast from melted stovepipes in molds made of soap. The course evolved gradually, again following the pattern of the original medieval process, with the first games being played haphazardly between the huts. In time, as the home-made equipment proliferated and more prisoners began to play, the course became formalized, nine holes with "browns" of packed sand, bunkers, and contoured

approaches. Eventually parcels from home brought real clubs and proper balls, and golf at Stalag Luft 3 caught up with the twentieth century. Tuition was organized for learners, exhibitions were arranged by the hotshot players, and a championship was held.

The severest penalty in the history of golf faced the man who played a loose shot. Anyone stepping over the rail which marked the inner perimeter was likely to be shot by the guards. In time the Germans came to adopt an attitude of uneasy tolerance and a white coat was issued to be worn as a mark of good faith that the wearer was simply retrieving a golf ball and not trying to escape. It was ironic that the Germans should have watched these harmless golfing activities with such mistrust. For under their noses one of the most daring escapes of the war was being engineered, via a tunnel dug under cover of a wooden vaulting horse. The Germans barely gave the vaulters a second look.

With the spread of golf across the globe, there was only one more frontier for golf to conquer and that was outer space. And so, in due course, it happened. On a mission to the surface of the moon astronaut Alan Shepard astonished his earthly TV audience while performing official EVA, or extra-vehicular activity. The prospect of weightless golf proved altogether too tempting for him. He had a six-iron head fitted to his moon pick and smuggled a golf ball aboard his spacecraft. The encumbrance of a space suit did not do much for his swing—indeed, you could say his first attempt was an air-shot, except that there is no air on the moon. Before the lunar dust had settled he took another swipe and gave a cry of satisfaction as the ball flew off under the effortless restraint of only one-sixth of the earth's gravity. For distance, Shepard's 900-yard drive humbles the boasts of every long-ball hitter to date. Those of us who could not be dragged within a mile of a space capsule can envy him that one supreme chance for one-upmanship.

5 · secrets of the great

courses

ne of the attractions of golf, some would even say its main charm, is that it is nearly always played in beautiful surroundings. There are some unattractive courses, generally unnecessarily so, since almost any open area can be transformed by imaginative use of trees. Golf can be a dreary experience if the course is little more than an open field in the middle of a heavily developed area. Trudging up and down parallel fairways at such places we miss the feeling of remoteness and being "away from it all" which should be part of the game. Golf after all is a form of escapism and it helps if we really can escape from the sight and sound and consciousness of our everyday worlds.

Out of sight, out of mind is a precept which green committees should keep constantly in mind. And if, therefore, a member's course happens to border the grounds of an ugly factory, he should lose no time in agitating for a screen of trees to be planted along that boundary. Never mind if it makes a fairway rather too narrow for comfort, or that he will not live to enjoy the full benefit of the improvement. His children will appreciate his foresight, and if in the meantime he has to take an iron off the tee to keep his ball in play, he can enjoy the masochistic delights of recalling his part in creating a "monster."

From the aesthetics of golf we can now turn to the golfing requirements of individual holes. This subject illustrates, but fails to explain, one idiosyncrasy common to the majority of golf-club members, namely, that nearly everyone believes his course a good one. Perhaps it is the result of natural community pride, and probably there is an element of self-deception as well. After all, no one would care to admit that anything about his golf was bad. Members like to think of their courses as being difficult but fair. Visitors are constantly being asked to agree that this is a "pretty good course," or that such is a particularly fine hole. And we visitors, with the politeness which is the obli-

gation of the guest, always agree. Yet if the proud member is taxed with the question, "Why do you say this is a good course?" or, "Why do you consider this a good hole?" the answer, as often as not, suggests quite the opposite. "We had a bunch of pros down here last summer for an exhibition and not one of them made par at that fourteenth." Such a statement merely implies that there is something wrong with the 14th. The difficulty is that no two golfers agree on what constitutes "good" or "bad" in golf courses. These are emotive words and hardly appropriate to the subject, but since they are the common coinage of golf discussions, let us by all means continue to use them after having first agreed what they mean.

At once we must discard the convention of visualizing a golf shot in terms of a line. It is all very well to stand on a tee and mentally plot a shot: "I will hit my drive from here to there, and then I will play my second from there to the green." That process involves two lines which, alas, all too often prove illusory. You set yourself up to aim, say, 4 yards left of a fairway bunker. How often does the shot follow that ideal path? Even if you are the world's straightest driver, your drives will deviate somewhat either side of the target. Actually, most of us can delete that comfortable word "somewhat" and substitute something like "considerably." The architect must think of us all. So he forgets about lines and works in angles. For the sake of discussion, let us take ten degrees, which is a pretty thin slice of pie but a generous enough angle for golfers. The architect may consider that a golfer with a driver in his hand should be able to hit his shots within five degrees either side of the perfect line. He can now draw a ten-degree arc on his plan and any area outside that arc is fair game for punishment in the form of light rough. He may now superimpose another arc, say twenty degrees, although in practice that would be highly benevolent, and the land outside this second arc may be severely punitive, with heavy rough,

Preceding pages: Pebble Beach's famous
7th hole whose 120 yards across the tip of peninsula
may require a wedge or anything up to
a wood, depending upon the mood of the weather.

132

trees, water, or boundary fences. All this may seem pretty basic, and so it is in relation to the drive, but when we come to consider the second shot, the principle of working in angles becomes more important.

The architect now starts from the area where a decent but not outstandingly long drive will come to rest. This time, on a two-shot hole, his ten-degree arc will govern the size of the green. Naturally, the greater the distance the bigger the target must be in order to cover the ten degrees of the arc. And it is here, in the second shot, that we can generally make a judgment as to whether we are playing a "bad" hole. Certainly, if we have hit a good drive and then have less than five degrees of leeway either side of the perfect second shot, we are entitled to feel that the hole is not entirely fair. Don't forget that for a first-class player it ought to be normal, not the exception, to hit the green in regulation figures under good conditions. Right. We golfers now have what amounts to a bill of rights. As long as we hit the ball far enough off the tee and within that ten-degree arc, we should expect to avoid trouble. In practice, almost every golf hole affords a much larger area of trouble-free fairway.

This is where the cunning of the architect comes into play. Very often he will provide the wide-open spaces, but if he is a good architect he will have made sure that the ten-degree principle operates. He will have contoured the hole in such a manner that the second shot must be played from a certain area on the fairway. And if you are outside that optimum area, you may have a perfect lie and be able to see the green, but you won't have a ten-degree arc to play through.

An entire book could be devoted to the subject of putting greens. And remarkably dull it would be: informative, but boring. In many instances the greens are the most distinctive mark of the architect, his signature if you like. Robert Trent Jones, the fashionable and successful (and, at times, superbly skillful) American architect, is noted for the size and eccentric shaping of his greens. (He is also notable for one of the most elegant responses to criticism in the history of golf. His short 4th hole over a pond at Baltusrol, New Jersey, is justly famous, but at first it was felt by the club to be unfairly difficult. Jones was summoned for a consultation. On the tee he scanned the scene across the pond and listened patiently while the shortcomings of the hole were explained to him. Then he took a club, dropped a ball, and holed his tee shot! Words were unnecessary.)

In the opinion of some golfing "graphologists," the Jones signature became excessively flowery in his later courses. These things are a matter of taste. But we can assert that very pronounced contouring of a green is unfair practice and often a tacit admission by the architect that he has failed to provide sufficient interest and challenge from tee to green. Plunging gradients on a green are an abomination and a defiance of the essence of golf, which is power allied to subtlety. The green is one area of the course where the architect must leave his work (and reputation) in the hands of other people. Having shaped it, and provided adequate drainage and irrigation, he departs. Now the greenkeeping staff takes over and it can quickly ruin the job. Standards of greenkeeping vary widely from course to course, and the condition of a green is much more important than its conformation. A good head greenkeeper is a treasure beyond price. Once a club has found such a man the committee should not hesitate to use blackmail, bribery, or the procurement of beautiful women to retain him.

As with the game itself, Americans, having learned course design from foreigners, have now become preeminent in the field. Traditionalists claim that new American courses are artificial—and that may be literally true in some cases. But is that so bad? Given the unpromising material with which the architects have to work, flat acres of scrub or wooded

wasteland, the result must be artificial if it is to succeed as a golf course. Of course, an undulating green layout with trees and manmade lakes is incongruous in a flat desert, but it is hardly out of place. The wonder is that it is there at all. Given a large enough budget and a blend of imagination and technique, a golf course can be built anywhere. And to call the result "artificial" is as absurd as criticizing the Taj Mahal for not being a mud hut.

The first requirement of a golf hole is that it be playable, which sounds so obvious as to be not worth mentioning. Remember, though, that golfers of every caliber, from the lordly pro down to the novice, must be able to play the hole. So if the architect provides a 170-yard carry across water from the tee, he will have made a hole which is unplayable for a segment of the golfing community, even though it may pro-

duce the simplest of challenges for stronger players. The 16th hole at Merion is a case in point. The second shot here is over a quarry and long enough to put the green out of range for some players even if they lay up to the very brink of hell. The solution which has been provided—and it can hardly be described as satisfactory—is a "ladies' aid," a detour of mown fairway around the quarry, turning the hole into a rather uninspiring par-6.

Those who practice the black arts of golf-course architecture are well versed in trickery and they know the occult powers water possesses. Water creates a neurosis in golfers. The very thought of this harmless fluid robs them of their normal powers of rational thought, turns their legs to jelly, and produces a palsy of the upper limbs, in much the same way as other liquid affects them at the 19th hole. Architects

For green, read brown: Oiled sand is the putting surface on the grounds of Morro Castle, Puerto Rico. Opposite: Example of the penal school of sandtrapping, 15th hole at National Golf Links, Long Island.

134

use these occult properties of water to telling advantage. The commonest method, and by far the most effective, is to present the golfer with an oblique view of the water hazard, so that he may be playing across the corner of a lake. That is to say, instead of confronting the player with a direct shot over water, the architect offers him a series of options, playing on the golfer's fears and greed in the hope that he will be of two minds when he hits the ball. And, as we all know, indecision is the most destructive attitude in golf. How many times have we cursed a bad shot when in fact we were never really sure what shot we were trying to play?

So we look out across the water and try to calculate distances (itself a difficult process over water) and decide how much of the corner we can safely cut. Nongolfers are incapable of understanding our problem. They argue that since a player is looking at the ball when he hits it, he cannot see the water and this should be a case of "out of sight, out of mind." What blissful ignorance! Those of us who try to play the game know that we cannot entirely dismiss the water from our thoughts, no matter how hard we concentrate on the process of swinging. The germinal fear directs our muscles. No matter how hard we try, unless we are very good players indeed, we involuntarily steer the shot away from the water, and this is why we seldom make really flush contact with the ball when there is water to be negotiated.

Experience reassures us that we hit our drives, say, 200 yards. Experience of a more bitter nature further tells us that when there is water about we make a mess of the shot. The temptation to look up prematurely to allay our anxieties all too often ruins the shot and simply confirms our secret fears. An architect does not need a fearsome expanse of water to play havoc with a golfer's subconscious. A narrow stream is enough if it is employed with cunning.

Again, the best holes are those which avoid a direct confrontation; instead of the stream running square across the fairway, it is much more effective if it crosses at a diagonal. This immediately sets up a conflict in the golfer's mind. Should he try to carry the stream at its nearest point? What if he tops the shot? No, perhaps it would be safer to play down the side where the water is farthest from him. Here, however, the fairway is tapering to a point and the longer the shot the more accurate it must be.

The 17th at Carnoustie is one of the more notorious finishing holes in championship golf. Here the Barry Burn winds to and fro across the fairway, effectively turning the hole into three islands. For the burn not only crosses the fairway but in strategic places it runs alongside as well. When the wind blows, as it frequently does with great force on Scotland's east coast, it is one of the truly intimidating challenges in golf. This hole has been the scene of many dramatic turns of fortune, but what was perhaps the biggest potential reverse proved an anticlimax.

In the Open Championship of 1968, the fourth round eventually resolved itself into a two-man struggle between Gary Player and Jack Nicklaus. After driving out of bounds at the 6th, Nicklaus seemed to have put himself out of the hunt, but by the time they reached the 17th tee there were only two shots in it to Player's advantage. Those two long final holes at Carnoustie are endowed with enough trouble to furnish an entire golf course, with the burn snaking all over, knee-high rough, out-of-bounds, and lavish acres of sand traps. A two-shot lead with two to play is not enough insurance to silence your jangling nerves at any time, but at Carnoustie it means less than ever. This was just the situation to inspire Nicklaus to throw off his natural caution and let rip. His drive at the 17th was awesome in its power. Seldom before can a golf ball have been struck harder. That drive cleared everything, contemptuously flying the dreaded burn and coming to rest less than 100 yards from the green.

The Improved Ladies' Tee

Special Golf-Links for Short-Sighted Players

Player, who is no slouch himself when it comes to driving, also hit a good one, just short of the last twist in the burn. He had a long-iron shot to the green, while Nicklaus had a three-quarter pitch with his wedge. Club for club, then, it was odds-on for a Nicklaus eagle against a regular birdie for Player. If Nicklaus could get back a stroke here he had every chance of catching Player on the 18th, because with his extra power he could hit the green with an iron, while Player would need two good woods. Probably these thoughts were running through Nicklaus's mind as he addressed himself to that short pitch. At all events it was not a very good one. By his standards it was downright sloppy. The shot came up short, leaving him a long putt from the front of the green. Both men made fours and now, with his two-shot lead intact, Player was able to take an iron off the 18th tee and play the hole for a safe and winning 5.

This incident illustrates another element which is necessary, or desirable at the least, in a golf hole: It should combine a potential for disaster with an equal potential for reward. And the two should be closely associated. In other words, the golfer with the skill and nerve to gamble for the reward—by cutting off the corner of a dogleg, for instance—should be exposed to the severest penalties if he fails.

One of the most famous holes in the world, and deservedly so, is the 16th at Cypress Point, California, which combines all the elements required for golfing excellence. It is spectacularly beautiful and is probably the most photographed hole in the world. By the yardstick that a great hole attacks the golfer even before he takes a club from the bag, this one has few equals. Most handicap players are beaten by this one before they play it. Stepping onto that tee, with the ocean crashing against the rocks below and the sea lions honking derision, the golfer is a tumult of emotions. Fear, awe, admiration, and indecision fight for supremacy. The hole is obviously playable; there is an easy, though cowardly, inland route by which the fainthearted may approach that daunting green set on a promontory. But there is also the prospect (unless the wind is especially unfavorable) of hitting over the inlet straight at the flag. It will have to be a good

Golf has been a staple source of fun for Punch, the British magazine, and these two examples were reprinted in New York in anthology Mr. Punch on the Links *in 1929.*

one, but if it succeeds the golfer can bask in the glorious memory of the moment for the rest of his life. Nowhere is he offered the chance of a richer prize or a more enormous failure. It is quite possible to stand on that tee and hit ball after ball into the Pacific, and many a man has done so. On the other hand, Bing Crosby can look back and reflect that his life has not been in vain, even if he discounted all the triumphs of his career, simply on the grounds that he once made a hole-in-one here.

Another rule-of-thumb measurement for a good hole is that it should inspire the power of total recall, even if played years before, and then only once. This 16th is certainly unforgettable, although the memory is challenged by numerous other examples from the treasure house of golf of the Monterey peninsula.

A common weakness on many holes is to site the most difficult hazards in places where they will catch only the worst shots. If a golfer duck-hooks his tee shot and squirts the ball only 150 yards, and wildly

off line in the bargain, he will have provided his own punishment in most cases. The green will be out of range for him, anyway, and it is rather rubbing his nose in it if his ball is tangled in deep rough as well.

Many courses have too much rough, especially some of the seaside links in the British Isles. For the indifferent player, golf on such courses can be misery. Every wayward shot finishes in thickly tangled grass from which—if you can find the ball at all—you have no other course but to chip back to the fairway. The purpose of golf, after all, is to provide enjoyment for all, good and bad player alike, and a hole which can only be tackled by a superior golfer is a bad hole.

There are, however, bad holes and bad holes. There is no excuse for the unplayable hole, but a case can be made for certain categories of bad hole. In fact, when we speak of bad holes it might be said that every course should have at least one. One weakness of the Augusta National course is that it lacks a rank bad hole. That apparently contradictory statement

Hazardous golf: The golfer must run a gauntlet of sand on the 6th at Seminole in Florida, which Ben Hogan called the best par-4 in the world. Beware water at the Williamsburg Inn course in Virginia.

needs clarifying, and for further enlightenment we must now change our viewpoint. Instead of looking at courses from the architect's standpoint, think in terms of the golfer. For the man who plays the game, golf holes can be divided into four categories: the hole which looks easy and is easy; the hole which looks easy but is difficult; the hole which looks and is difficult; and the hole which looks difficult and is easy.

For our purposes of providing a "bad" hole for every course, we must go to the first category and seek a pushover hole, one that plays as easily as it looks. It can take many forms, possibly a short par-3 with a generous green, or a 300-yarder with a wide fairway and no trouble to speak of. Essentially, it is a hole where our firing arc has given us a much wider margin for error than usual and which makes no great demands on length. It is, then, what we tend to dismiss in our lofty way as "a nothing hole." And that is exactly how the architect wants us to think of it; indeed, that we should not think about it at all. Here at last is a hole where we can just tee up and let fly, where par is a matter of routine. Coming in the middle of a good course which has taxed our powers of concentration it is a relief to arrive at a hole with no niggling worries about bunkers or trees, and where all we have to think about is hitting the ball. There is no catch in it. The hole is a pushover and we move on with that deliciously smug feeling of having got the game licked.

This momentary euphoria is exactly what the architect planned to induce. And if he is a good architect—which is to say an evil, conniving genius—he will follow his nothing hole with an example from the second category: a hole which looks easy but is difficult. The poor deluded golfer, still glowing with arrogance from his success at the previous hole, will hit off with the same abandon. And then the trap is sprung. The most elegant victory an architect can contrive is to produce a situation where the golfer comes to grief with a good shot. Life offers few more superbly ludicrous sights than that of a good golfer hitting a full-blooded drive exactly as he intended and then watching his ball rattle into trees or plop into a lake.

How can such supreme idiocy be contrived? One method—and it is really a clumsy confidence trick—is to offset the tee at an angle. The golfer, like any other human, is about ninety percent sheep and if he is accustomed to playing from tees which are built in the direction of the target area, he becomes conditioned to setting up his stance square to the tee. Ninety-nine times out of a hundred that stance is also square to the fairway. Now, with the tee offset five degrees, confusion is created in his subconscious. The pattern of lines caused by the mower does not, for once, correspond with the direction of his shot. He may hit his usual shot in relation to the tee and drive straight off the fairway. More likely he will make an unconscious adjustment in his swing to compensate for the novel situation and hit across the ball.

The championship tee of the 8th hole at Royal Birkdale is lined up on the right rough, and that is exactly where many shots finish. This technique, one feels, borders on unfair practice, almost on the level of using blind holes and placing bunkers out of the golfer's sight.

The deception should be, and can be, more subtle. In the best cases it involves optical illusions. Every feature of the hole should be clearly in view, which is the architectural equivalent of the conjurer showing he has nothing up his sleeve. The illusionists make use of several natural peculiarities. An unbroken expanse of land, or water, with no bunkers or other landmarks to provide focusing references, always looks longer than the reality, especially if there is a slight brow, so the golfer cannot actually see the distant surface of the fairway. A hazard at 240 yards will appear to be well out of range. A depression in the ground has the reverse effect, and this is especially useful for playing havoc with a golfer facing a long

second shot to the green. The eye's depth perception is deceived by the hidden ground and the player can be tricked into under-clubbing, sometimes by as much as three clubs. It does not help to *know* that the green is 190 yards away. If it *looks* to be 150 yards the human mechanism will react to the visual evidence. Even if the golfer selects the right club, he will spare the shot, without any conscious intention of doing so, and come up short.

The other main optical illusion is created by a change of levels. Playing from an elevated tee everything looks nearer than it is, and the golfer from his commanding position overlooking the scenery feels stronger. Perhaps we can call this the Empire State Syndrome. If anyone doubts that it exists, it can easily be checked by a single experiment. Go onto the roof of a tall building and imagine yourself hitting a good drive, a real Sunday Special. Judge where this drive would finish. Now go down and pace off the length of that imaginary drive. It may surprise you to find that you have allowed yourself to believe that you could hit the first half-mile drive in history.

Hitting to an elevated green is equally confusing. Looking upward, the golfer feels insignificant and intimidated. It looks farther than it is. For architects, however, this particular illusion can be self-

In pragmatic approach to course design,
Bobby Jones plots what must be the most strategic
golf course in the world, during
building of Augusta National in 1932.

defeating, because although the golfer may be conned into taking one club too much, he is likely to lose distance through trying to hit the ball too hard. So he may end up pin high after all, although he may be wide of the green.

These, then, are the main tricks of the architect, employed with infinite variety and often unconsciously, for they are all tricks of nature rather than man. Many notable examples of golfing psychological warfare are accidents of nature, especially on the featureless, duneland courses of Scotland.

The last two categories of hole are largely self-explanatory. The hole which looks difficult and requires no explanation; it's too obvious a type. The commonest form of hole which looks difficult but in fact is easy has a tremendous hazard to strike terror into the heart of the golfer, but is so sited that it does not come into play for practical purposes. Although

it is physically irrelevant its presence impinges itself on the subconscious with damaging effect. A good example occurs on an otherwise undistinguished course near London. It is a short hole of 150 yards or so, so length is no problem, and the green is both expansive in size and benign by nature. However, directly in front of the tee there yawns an abyss, actually a disused quarry. Peering into its dark interior overgrown with brambles, you get the feeling that the golfer who ventured down those precipitous banks would be fortunate to emerge again, let alone play a successful recovery shot from that tangle of shrubbery. The quarry measures only about 100 yards across, so it should not come into the reckoning at all. Yet it exerts such a baleful influence on the fainthearted that in their anxiety to see the ball safely over the trouble, they look up too quickly—and top their shots into its ravening maw.

The sign to quicken the blood of any golfer and the realization (r.) which tests the strongest nerves, as the player drives the 12th over a wilderness of hidden bunkers.

One rather neglected element in modern golf architecture is the short par-4. These days the emphasis is on length, and yardage is too often taken as the criterion of greatness. Members speak with awe of holes nearly 600 yards long, but in truth these are often the dullest part of golf, particularly for better players. Frequently, the second shot calls for nothing more than forward motion. Just move it ahead and it makes very little difference whether this object is achieved by topping a driver along the ground or hitting a crisp three-iron.

The very expression "par-5" strikes a forbidding chord and the golfer flexes his muscles to meet the challenge to his virility. In fact, if we are thinking in terms of par, as we should be, most par-5s are the simplest holes on the course. A birdie can often be achieved with two indifferent shots and one good one, and the hole yields a par to three mis-hits. The standard of stroke-making needed for par-5s is lower than for any other type of hole, provided—and the qualification is all-important—that we are content to settle for a 5. What happens more often is that we approach these long holes with a vague ambition to get up in 2, although we would be hard put to defend that aim with rational argument. We try to hit that little bit harder, miss the drive, and then seek a miracle of recovery with subsequent shots.

Long par-4s are a much more testing proposition. These, too, lose their challenge if those of us who cannot make the distance accept that fact with grace and play them as three-shotters, taking advantage of our handicap strokes. Vanity, which shares with fear the doubtful distinction of being the golfer's worst enemy, all too often undoes us again. But the short par-4, of 300 yards or less, is well within everyone's range and offers scope for the architect to display his cunning. The best examples, employing the principles we have already discussed, should offer a good chance for a 3 to the player who can match his boldness with accuracy, but threatens him with a 6, or a 7, if he falters. The 9th on the Old Course at St. Andrews is an example, all the more extraordinary because at first sight it might qualify as one of our "nothing" holes. It is flat and wide and the green is not sculptured in any way, simply a prepared area of putting turf on the fairway. The hole is almost drivable and yet the second shot, the shortest of pitches most of the time, has been the undoing of many a fine player.

Another Scottish course, Turnberry, has a beauty, the 13th, and here the problem is quite different. After a good drive you have to pitch to a plateau green, an island elevated just high enough to play optical tricks and affect judgment of distance.

Possibly the most important convention of course architecture, so common that we rather take it for granted, is the dogleg. There are courses, mostly laid out by unqualified men working with restricted areas, which consist largely of dead-straight holes. Trudging up and down these drab fairways, often laid out in parallel, like sardines in a can, is the nearest experience to boredom golf has to offer. The pity of it is that often such unimaginative layout is unnecessary. A change of direction in the middle of a fairway makes all the difference in the world. The game is transformed in that a player must decide whether to gamble on cutting corners and risking trouble for the chance of a shorter second shot. And if the hole is bordered by trees there is the added bonus of changing vistas as you progress up the fairway. There is no excuse for dullness on a golf course when variety can be achieved so easily.

A fine example of ingenious use of the dogleg is seen at the east course of the Royal Melbourne Golf Club, whose two courses on the famous Melbourne sand belt must rank with the finest championship courses of the world. Here the boundary of the club's property is a straight fence imposing the necessity of a chain of straight holes. The architect solved this problem by planting stands of trees along the boundary, so that the tee shots are directed away from the fence. The result is a sequence of interesting holes and playing them one is not conscious of the out-of-bounds at all.

The deliberate use of out-of-bounds as hazards seems to many people to be a sign of weakness. Occasionally, it cannot be helped. St. Andrews and Troon, for instance, are bordered by railway lines which have the respectability of history to commend them. But another British championship course, Royal Liverpool at Hoylake, is confined in places by artificial out-of-bounds, mere trenches cut in turf banks, and this is surely a practice to be discouraged. After all, if we are going to stoop to these strategies, golf might as well be played over a flat field with the fairways marked out like a football pitch.

Most, though not all, architects agree that golf holes should be as natural as possible and fit into the landscape with as little disturbance as possible. The skill of the architect comes in the siting of trees and greens in such a way as to combine a golfing challenge with a natural setting. Nature is the real architect: Man simply makes a few minimal adjustments.

In fact, in these days of earthmoving machinery it matters little where a course happens to be built. The decisive factors are geology and climate. A wet and temperate climate is best—or, what amounts to the same thing, a temperate climate plus a good irrigation system. As to geology, the finest subsoil for golf is sand, or gravel, with good natural drainage. It supports fine-bladed grasses and the conifers—larch, spruce, and pines—which are a feature of so many excellent courses.

Seaside golf is highly regarded in Britain because of the springy turf; the only way you can get a bad lie on it is by the misfortune of landing in someone else's divot scrape. St. Andrews, Muirfield, Carnoustie, Troon, Old Prestwick, Royal Birkdale, Sand-wich, Royal Lytham and St. Anne's, Sunningdale, Walton Heath, and Westward Ho! all are built on sand, inland in some cases. Mostly they remain much as they were left by the receding tide ages ago, ridged and fissured by the sea, and now simply grown over with the most perfect turf you can imagine. The golf on these linksland courses can be a severe trial to a man who subscribes to the view that punishment should be the sanction for error. Play St. Andrews or Sandwich in a dry spell, when there is bone in the ground, and a perfectly hit drive to the center of the fairway can kick capriciously into the rough. This sort of experience is supposed to test a golfer's character. In the main it provides an impromptu display of his vocabulary.

There are exceptions. Muirfield, although undoubtedly by the sea, is a fair course if a difficult one, and by and large the golfer gets the due reward for his shots. As it is prepared for the Open Championship, such as when Jack Nicklaus failed with the third trick of his grand-slam attempt in 1972, it is tight and the greens are fast and hard. And if Nicklaus ever reflects on the part luck played in that Open it will concern the unbelievable good luck the winner, Lee Trevino, enjoyed in his last two rounds. By Trevino's own reckoning, he saved himself at least six strokes by hitting the flagstick with over-bold recoveries, holing out twice. When the fates are favoring one man to that degree it is impossible to prevail against him.

In America there are no links courses in the true sense of the expression. But there are sand courses, and none finer than Pine Valley, New Jersey. It is slightly specialized in its appeal, but given the ability to make 175-yard carries off the tee, Pine Valley's claim to be the best course in the world—a claim made on its behalf by enthusiastic visitors, rather than by the club itself—is not so preposterous. Some prefer to label it the most difficult course in the world, but this is a judgment which must be flavored according to the ability of the golfer. On his first visit Arnold

Tony Jacklin, playing alongside the railway at Royal Lytham and St. Anne's on way to his 1969 Open Championship, exhibits characteristic leg action. Below: The Windmill, Wimbledon, and the "Maiden" at Sandwich.

How nature can deceive the eye: Two examples of distorted depth-perception which makes clubbing difficult—over Royal Portrush's undulating wilds and at an elevated tee at Hermitage, Ireland.

Palmer beat par, for instance, and thereby won a large enough bet to buy an engagement ring and elope. The hazards are forbidding, but there is no law compelling a man to put his ball into a vast, unraked bunker or into the stands of pine bordering the fairways. It is a magnificent golf course, and a majestic one, which is something rather different, and it is all because of sand. Next time you curse the stuff as you flail away in a bunker, pause in your sweaty labors and reflect that those dastardly grains of crushed silica are the golfer's best friend. You may have to reflect rather hard, but it is true.

We have been discussing the golf architect's job solely in terms of strategic responsibilities, or what we might call the visionary side of his work. This is where he needs a special form of insight; indeed, in some cases genius would not be too extravagant a word. Most of us imagine we could lay out a golf course, and sometimes, when we come across a grassy promontory by an ocean bay and say "What a golf hole that would make," we might even be right. Only a fool could fail to recognize the obvious. But the architect may have to fight his way through thicket or gaze out over a flat wilderness of sandy scrub. That is when he needs his visionary powers to plot the course of the bulldozers. He also needs technical skills to cope with a multiplicity of problems of drainage, watering, and the cultivation of turf. But we need not concern ourselves here with the plumbing.

Our concern is to try and understand how the architect is plotting our downfall as golfers, so that perhaps we can foil him, or at least appreciate in retrospect the mastery of the man who has brought us to despair. We have examined the theory. Now let us browse over a few notable courses and see how the precepts of great architecture have been translated into practice. Where better to start than Augusta National, the beautiful and exacting monument to the greatest golfer of all time. Bobby Jones built Augusta with Dr.

Alistair Mackenzie, one of the supreme masters of his craft, who was also responsible for Royal Melbourne. Between them they produced a course which fulfills nearly all the qualifications. If one had to find a criticism of Augusta, it would be that it is too good. The concentration is too concentrated. The golfer who hopes to beat par has to apply himself singlemindedly on every shot. There is no let-up. If it had a "nothing hole" to provide a change of pace and break the player's concentration, it might be even more difficult.

Augusta is a good example of the strategic type of course, as opposed to the penal variety which depends for its difficulties on savage length and harsh penalties. The fairways of Augusta are as wide as you could wish, in the main, and the greens are large. For a good player par is not an exceptionally difficult target, easier than on most championship courses. The problems begin with ambitions to improve on par. It is not enough to hit the fairway with the drive. In order to set up a birdie chance the drive must be positioned with great accuracy and only then can an approach be made with any reasonable expectations of finishing near the hole, and on the preferred side of the hole. Just where the optimum areas on the fairway will be depends, of course, on the position of the hole. At Augusta, more so than on any other championship course, the siting of the pins must be taken into account while setting up for the drive. For the handicap golfer, with some concessions in length from the forward tees, Augusta is not unduly severe, although those fast and undulating greens frequently require three putts from the edge.

There is another important quality to Augusta which owes nothing to the architect or the physical layout of the course. Any golf course which has a long history of great events acquires a patina of awe. Only the dullest of golfers can fail to be affected by the realization that here Gene Sarazen had his famous double eagle and there is the pond in which

Ben Hogan's hopes were drowned.

At St. Andrews the ghosts of the mighty are even more populous and there is the added feeling, whether historically justified or not, that here is where it all began. It would be no exaggeration to say that many golfers approach St. Andrews with the reverence of pilgrims and that their games suffer accordingly. Many a fine player has thus been disappointed by his first experience on the Old Course, but nearly all of them grow to like the links over subsequent visits and are inspired by its historical vibrations. To contemporary eyes, it is hopelessly old-fashioned, with its vast double greens accommodating two holes, and its myriad bunkers, mostly with individual names and frequently hidden from view. For all that, the unprejudiced golfer who accepts St. Andrews for what it is, without bemoaning its unfairness or quaking at its reputation, can plot a route between the spattered pot bunkers just big enough, in Bernard Darwin's phrase, to hold an angry man and his mashie.

In the Open Championship of 1970, Tony Jacklin almost committed the sacrilege of taking St. Andrews apart. In the first round, playing late in the day, he was out in 29 and started back in the same birdie mood. Was the unthinkable about to happen, was the Old Course about to be humbled? A storm broke with savage fury, the round was suspended, and when Jacklin resumed in the gray dawn next morning, the spell was broken. At that time it was easy to believe that the flashing lightning and growling heavens were an act of supernatural intervention.

The caliber of a golf course must always be a personal assessment in some measure, depending on the degree of importance which the golfer puts on different features. Those of us who play purely for pleasure—if we took the trouble to analyze the sources of our enjoyment—would probably agree on the following priorities: (1) scenic beauty, (2) quality of turf and greens—which depends on the nature of the soil, (3) strategic layout of the holes, (4) incidental facilities, such as the quality of the clubhouse.

On that formula, Irish golf demands at least a footnote in any review of courses. This small country contains more superb courses than any area of comparable size. To explain the special appeal of Irish golf we must return to an original thought that half the appeal of the game is "getting away from it all." Ballybunion, Portmarnock, Lahinch, and Portrush are rugged links. Inland there is Killarney, ringed by purple mountains and set at the side of vast lakes. The setting is almost too beautiful, especially when the air carries the opiate scent of peat smoke.

If these are the jewels of Irish golf there are also many semiprecious stones, indifferent courses, and downright bad ones. But to continue the metaphor, Irish golf is unpolished. The stones have not been faceted and tricked up with the frills of modernity. The golfer gets the feeling that this is how golf used to be—and how it ought to be. Remote and primitive on a tee at Ballybunion, with the Atlantic crashing below and the wind stinging his face, the golfer can imagine that the world we call civilization does not exist.

And, what's more, for the moment the courses are not overrun by visiting hordes and infected by golf's most stultifying disease, the obligatory five-hour tourist round. No matter how well God and the architect may have done their work, the pleasure of the game must ultimately come from within the golfer. The Mountains of Mourne may sweep down to the sea; the ball may sit up as prettily as you could wish on the fine grass; and the shot may be as inviting as you ever dreamed. All these are as nothing if you have to wait five minutes on every shot while a four-ball in front blithely disregards all the canons of golfing etiquette and the natural laws of good manners. The final element in golf-course architecture, then, is the golfer himself, the player who respects the course and who allows others to take pleasure from it.

merica is for winners. The idea that all men are born free and equal may be honored in constitutional theory, but in practical terms it is to many people a thoroughly spurious notion. Whether or not every American child starts from the same mark, he is quickly involved in a competitive society which measures success in terms of outdoing others. To neutral outsiders it sometimes seems this emphasis on success, which has created the richest nation on earth, is unduly hard on losers. It was an American who said, "Nobody remembers who came in second." It may be a sentimental reaction, or even socialistic, but that remark seems to call for the response, "What a pity." Losers, after all, are essential to winners.

While society rewards its winners with wealth and respect, the nation, clinging to the ideal of equality, makes no official recognition of success. Arnold Palmer may be invited to dine at the White House, but if he had been born in a different country we can imagine that such an invitation would include a tap on the shoulder and the command, "Arise, Sir Arnold." One exception to this official disdain of honors is New York City's splendid practice of the ticker-tape parade. Such a parade, with marching bands and cheering crowds, took place in the summer of 1930.

The triumphant hero was a stocky young Georgian, Robert Tyre Jones, who had just returned from winning the British Open and the Amateur Championships. These days such a "double" would perhaps not be quite such a remarkable achievement. It takes no flight of fancy to imagine the golf coach at some university finding a young Jack Nicklaus with the potential to do it. But in 1930 the situation was very different. Jones had proved himself the outstanding golfer of his era. He had won the U.S. Amateur title four times and taken three national Open titles, and on two previous occasions he had beaten the best British professionals, which at that time meant the best in the

world, for the Open Championship.

The gulf between professional and amateur was not so wide in those days as it now is. The British amateurs, Roger Wethered and Cyril Tolley, were fine players and quite capable of beating anyone, especially over the short sprint of an eighteen-hole match in the Amateur Championship. That year it was played over the Old Course at St. Andrews, where on an earlier visit Jones had torn up his card in disgust and further signaled his opinion of the place by teeing up his ball and deliberately driving it into the sea. Over the years Jones came to respect and love the Old Course. He wrote: "Truly, if I had to select one course upon which to play the match of my life, I should have selected the Old Course." As it happened, this is exactly the ordeal he faced in 1930, for after narrowly surviving the preliminaries he came up against Tolley in a semifinal round.

It was to prove one of the great matches of all time. To read Jones' account of "the completely brutal ferocity of that man-to-man contest" is to bring home how insipid stroke-play golf is compared to a good match. This is not the place for hole-by-hole detail. Suffice to say that Tolley squared the match at the 16th, and then occurred the incident which provokes argument to this day. Jones' second to the notorious road hole hit a spectator. The question is whether it would otherwise have carried onto the road, which surely would have cost him the match. If's and but's do not count in golf. Jones halved the hole and the next. And he won the 19th to take the match. "It was the kind of match," he said, "in which each player plays himself so completely out that at the end the only feeling to which he is sensitive is one of utter exhaustion."

A measure of luck is necessary for any champion, and if the spectator at the 17th had indeed provided a stroke of fortune for Jones, it was nothing compared to the chance that this match took place in the afternoon. If it had been played in the morning and

Jones had been required to play another match the same day, he must surely have been beaten. As it was, he had a night's sleep in which to recover his strength and restore his competitive fires. And the title, after a final against Wethered, was his. The first quadrant of the Grand Slam was successfully achieved.

The Open Championship followed at Hoylake on the flat and uninspiring links course of the Royal Liverpool golf club. In the last round Jones was in contention, and for the first time that week he played the opening holes in respectable figures. He felt that a reasonable score probably would be good enough to win the title.

Then, at the 480-yard 8th, he took a 7 in what he described as "the most reasonable manner possible." Every golfer has suffered the experience of running up a big score without playing a bad shot and that is just what happened. A good drive was followed by a solid spoon shot which just missed the left edge of the green. The ball lay on the fairway some 20 yards from the hole with no intervening obstacles other than a brow. Jones had to get his ball up the slope and then stop it quickly on the green, which fell away quite steeply. Anxious not to run too far past the hole on the fast downslope, he chipped short by a foot or so and the ball did not make the green. He chipped again, still conscious of the danger that the ball could roll well past the hole—and left it ten feet short. His putt went a foot past and then he hurried the tap-in and missed it.

That body blow knocked all tactical thoughts from Jones' head. It was, he said, no longer a case of attacking or defending. His only idea was to go on hitting the ball as best he could and get the round finished. And that he did. Another stroke of luck came when a wayward drive rebounded kindly from a steward's head. Jones finished in orderly fashion and with no real threat from the opposition. Two tricks of the Grand Slam were his after the hardest championship of his life. He had earned his ticker-tape welcome.

The U.S. Open that year was played at Interlachen, Minneapolis, and began on the hottest day Jones could remember. (He was so saturated with perspiration at the end of the round that his tightly knotted tie had to be cut free with a knife.) The golf, at least, was not quite so feverish. Jones had a five-stroke lead after three rounds and for a player of his caliber such a margin was enough to cushion him against the inevitable faltering of the last round. Macdonald Smith's brave challenge was, as it had been at Hoylake, not quite strong enough. Three tricks.

At this point we may perhaps pause for a moment of idle conjecture. Let us make some fairly sweeping assumptions and put ourselves in Jones' position at this period. Here we are, the finest player in the world, poised on the brink of the greatest challenge that golf has to offer, the Grand Slam. What would we have done? Most of us, surely, would have taken a short rest and then launched into an intensive program of preparation for the final ahead. Jones did nothing of the kind and this illustrates more clearly than anything the remarkable qualities of the man. He was a real amateur in the sense that he played golf for fun. For the moment he had played enough and went home, back to his law office to work, and to play an occasional social game with his friends at East Lake, Atlanta. Jones was not exactly complacent about his prospects in the U.S. Amateur Championship (he never undertook any major golf event lightly or with any other intention than of winning it), but he realized that over 36 holes of match play he could expect to beat the best that amateur golf could offer in opposition.

The championship was held at Merion. The highly strung Jones was assailed by doubts and fears during the week, but these arose mainly from the tension of the situation rather than from the quality of the opposition. Each round was a triumphal progress and the final a formality. The Grand Slam was his, sealing the greatest golfing career of all time. In seven years

he had won thirteen major championships and finished second six times. It is possible that the record of thirteen championships will be surpassed and that another Grand Slam, in its modern form, will be achieved. However, it is inconceivable that anyone will do it in the Jones style, as a weekend amateur who often put his clubs away for months at a time. During his fourteen years of competitive golf, Jones studied for examinations and took honors degrees in law, English, and engineering. He also worked at his legal practice. For him golf was a diversion and when he completed the Grand Slam he retired.

Although he had withdrawn from the lists, Jones' contributions to golf were by no means over. With his friend Clifford Roberts he constructed the Augusta National, incorporating many of the ideas he formulated from playing championship courses and creating what is probably the finest inland course in the world. And here he instituted an annual tournament for his friends, which grew into the Masters, one of the elements of the modern Grand Slam. He died in 1971 of a wasting spinal disease which had kept him a cripple since middle age. The records may fade, but

Bob Jones' memorial in the azaleas and towering Georgia pines of Augusta will surely endure as long as golf is played.

Although Jones played with hickory-shafted clubs, in almost every other respect he could be classified among the moderns. He was certainly a modern player in style and outlook. On that basis we would have to consider Harry Vardon as the first of the moderns, even though he played mainly with hickory shafts and the guttie ball. Incidentally, in one respect Vardon was uncompromisingly old-fashioned, even though he could well be called the father of modern golf. He refused to have anything to do with the method of attaching a shaft to the head of a driver by gluing it into a socket bored into the neck, which had become universal practice during his early career. He insisted that the old way was best, that is to say, a tapered shaft glued to a similarly tapered neck and firmly bound with twine for the entire length of this splice, or "scare." Vardon maintained that a scared driver was a better union of shaft and head, and consequently gave him better control of his drives. Perhaps it did. Or perhaps it was a case of wishful thinking, a

Above: Wood-faced irons to cushion shock of stonelike guttie balls (l.), and early nineteenth-century master woods.
Opposite: Developing ideas, including rubber-faced pitching club (l.) and first metal shaft, 1914 (r.).

common habit among golfers at all levels. It does not matter, because the result was the same. When it comes to a golfer and his clubs, faith is more important than fact. The man who believes his driver to be perfect, makes it so. And conversely, believing a club to be "wrong," particularly putters, makes the most scientifically perfect implement useless.

In those days of handmade clubs, a golfer might swing two hundred mashies before he found one with the right feel. Those were the days of mysticism. Legends say that these early masters had such sensitive touch that the sets they laboriously collected were later found by modern scientific measurement to be perfectly "matched." In fact, such sets, like those of Bobby Jones, were found to vary widely in swing weight from club to club. Whether this is due to fallibility in Jones' touch or to shortcomings in the swingweight system is an open question.

Nowadays Vardon is remembered mainly for giving his name to the commonest method of gripping the club, with the little finger of the right hand overlapping the left forefinger. The Vardon grip is, by almost universal consent, the correct grip. In fact, Vardon did not invent the method at all. It had been used by other players; Vardon's place in the story was to make it popular. He was for years the finest player in

the world, and as such it was natural for golfers to copy everything about his method. Actually, Vardon did employ a unique grip on occasions. When faced with a short chip shot and anxious not to drag the ball to the left by having the right hand overpower the stroke, he sometimes overlapped the last two fingers of his right hand. This kept the left hand in control of the stroke and the clubface square to the target.

The real contribution to golf of this Channel Islander, who won the British Open six times and the U.S. Open once, was the standard he set in method. Before Vardon, golf was a power game. Players clenched their clubs with two-fisted grips and with the right hand well under the shaft. They spread their feet wide apart to anchor their tackety boots firmly to the earth, and they whacked into that little ball. Style as we know it today meant nothing. Golfers used whatever method seemed appropriate and no one thought the worse of him for unorthodoxy. Many players stood very open to allow themselves an uninhibited bash.

Golf at this time was played in two distinct phases. A player used distance clubs for getting into the vicinity of the target and then accuracy clubs to play to the green. The function of the wooden clubs was to move the ball forward as far as possible in the hope that it would not stray off line too far for a shot to the green. It is easy to imagine the impact of Vardon's arrival on the golfers of the day. The brawny giants who made the earth shake with the fury of their striking were joined by the slight figure of the self-

Great amateurs: Britain's Cyril Tolley (opposite), and Bobby Jones (above l.) talking to the man who founded U.S. Amateur Championship and won inaugural event, Charles Macdonald. Small photo shows Jones' classic grip.

The Immortal Bobby, winner of his third U.S.
Open at Winged Foot; Jones playing during first leg of his
Grand Slam, the 1930 British Amateur
Championship at St. Andrews, and with hero's escort.

taught professional who stood lightly to the ball, like a soldier "at ease," and gripped the club gently in the fingers. With a deceptively smooth and rhythmic swing following through to a well-balanced pose facing the target, he whisked the ball past the musclemen and straight up the *middle* of the fairway. What a revelation! Vardon may not have been the first to try combining distance with accuracy, but he was the first to succeed. He did not hope to "get up" with his brassie; he expected to hit the ball near the hole—and he did so. By experiment Vardon also discovered how to control his shots without sacrificing length. The exacting new standards he brought to golf could not be denied. You could not slug it out in this company.

It was necessary to study Vardon and

copy him. From him, then, came the idea that style was important, that percentage golf paid off, and that practice and dedication were essential for the golfer who hoped to compete at this game of accuracy allied with power. The new golf had arrived and Harry Vardon was its high priest. He made several visits to the United States and was in great demand for exhibitions. Golfers flocked to watch him, hoping to discover the secret of his method.

Another legend grew about Vardon's accuracy. It was said that when he played two rounds on the same day, so great was his precision that in the afternoon round he would hit the ball out of his morning divots. Extravagant nonsense, of course, but the fact that such a story gained general currency tells us

Broadway hailed the conqueror (in second car) after he won the British Amateur and Open Championships in 1930. Above: Jones, with wife Mary behind him, at City Hall with Mayor Jimmy Walker.

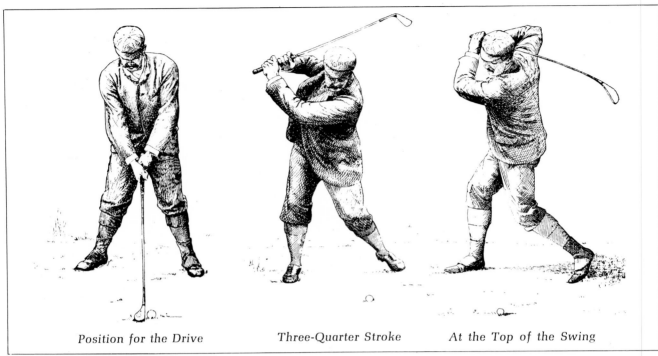

| Position for the Drive | Three-Quarter Stroke | At the Top of the Swing |

something about the reputation of this taciturn man. Another story—this one with the virtue of authenticity —tells how Vardon, being engaged to hit golf shots in the sports department of a large store, relieved the boredom of this sterile exercise by aiming at the valve of the fire-sprinkler system. He hit it so regularly that the manager feared his store would be flooded and begged Vardon to stop.

It is impossible to think of Vardon without recalling two golfers whose names were linked with his: J. H. Taylor and James Braid. Taylor was a West Countryman who grew up on the breezy links of Westward Ho! in Devon and developed the wide, sweeping style so often associated with seaside golfers. J. H. was quick-witted and quick-tempered at times. He was a small bird-like man in contrast to James Braid, a large man in every sense. If Vardon was an artist, and the term is perhaps not too fanciful, then

Taylor and Braid were superb craftsmen. In Braid's case this was literally true, for he began life in his native Scotland as a joiner. He moved to England as a clubmaker and soon won a reputation as a fine golfer and a man of extraordinary personal qualities. We can see from contemporary accounts and early photographs that both Taylor and Braid modified their styles and their grips over the years, and there can be no doubt that it was Vardon's example which prompted the changes. Among them these three players dominated British golf before World War I. The newspapers christened them, somewhat ponderously, the Great Triumvirate. Between 1891 and 1914 they won sixteen championships, and Taylor was the major inspiration in organizing the Professional Golfers' Association.

Vardon transformed golf and Taylor contributed to the improvement of the professional's lot. Braid's place in the history of the game is secure for

Golf instruction of 1892, which may explain the tradition of drowning one's disappointments in strong drink. Opposite: Engraving by W. Dendy Sadler, "A Winter Evening"—dreaming of spring, no doubt.

162

the thrilling eloquence of his play and the style of the man himself. Few professionals have been so well loved as the tall Scot. As professional at Walton Heath he was in great demand as a playing companion by visiting politicians. In such company a man who listened politely and hardly spoke a word would indeed be popular.

On his visits to America Vardon traveled with Ted Ray, a stolid and powerful professional of the old school, who hit the ball prodigious distances. Ray was never the equal of the Triumvirs, although he did win one Open and tied (with Vardon and Francis Ouimet) for the U.S. Open one year. He was, however, a congenial companion, and for American spectators it must have been particularly instructive to watch Vardon and Ray together. Between them they epitomized the two extremes of golf, the rapier and the broadsword, or the artist and the artisan. A contrast in styles makes for added interest in a golf match, as in any sporting encounter, and doubtless this element was one of the reasons why Vardon liked to have Ray with him.

Before the period of the Great Triumvirate, that is to say, through the turn of the century, there had been many fine professionals, although in the matter of the development of golf, no one of them was particularly more significant than the other. Old Tom Morris and his son, Young Tom, whose bearded faces figure prominently in so many golfing prints in the world's clubhouses, made the Open Championship

'Twas ever thus—the craftsmen made the equipment and then the crafty men of the advertising world set out to beguile the customers with seductive promises and bargains in the public prints.

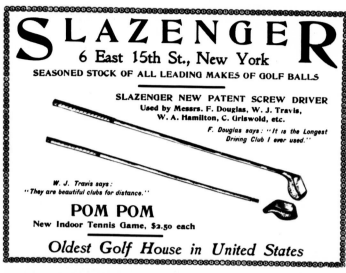
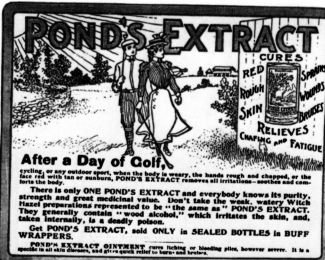

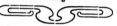

something of a family affair in its early years.

By all accounts, including the judgment of Tom Senior, who may have been prejudiced, Young Tom was the more accomplished player. In the mythology of golf he certainly commands the greater attention, since he died before reaching his prime. His wife died in childbirth while Tom was away from St. Andrews playing golf, and his father kept the news from him until they were returning home. Young Tom fell into a deep melancholy and shortly afterward followed his wife to the grave. We do not know how good a player Young Tom was. The reports are sketchy and the scores tell us little, since Scottish coastal golf is so

greatly affected by the weather. Young Tom won his third championship belt, ancestor of the silver jug which is now the Open trophy, with a two-round score of 149 in 1870. Since he won it three times in succession, it became his personal property. We may be tempted to draw exaggerated conclusions from the fact that ten years previously the winning score had been twenty-five strokes higher, an average of twelve shots a round worse. However, as visitors to Scotland will know, it is quite possible for conditions to vary by as much as ten strokes a round. All we can say, then, is that the Morrises were the best players around during their day.

These days the professional golfer is inclined to see his predecessors as servile creatures. Yet in terms of social advancement the nineteenth century was a period of considerable progress. The first professionals were caddies who were capable of playing when the occasion arose. Gentlemen golfers were warned not to tip their caddies generously since these rascals would certainly dissipate their money on drink. For their own good, caddies had to be kept firmly in their place. As late as 1900 the golf historian Horace Hutchinson wrote: "The professional, as we are now chiefly acquainted with him, is a 'feckless,' reckless, creature. In the golfing season in Scotland he makes his money all the day, and spends it all the night. His sole loves are golf and whisky. He works at odd times—job work or time work—in the shops; but he only does it when reduced to an extremity. If he were but ordinarily thrifty, he could lay by in the autumn sufficient to carry him on through the season of his discontent, when no golf is. He can lightly earn seven and sixpence a day by playing two rounds of golf; or, if he does not get an engagement, three and sixpence a day by carrying clubs. These are about the fees paid at St. Andrews and Musselburgh, Scotland, which are the great manufactories of the professionals who go forth to many links as green-keepers. . . . In the medal weeks

When British golf was supreme. Left to right: James Braid, J. H. Taylor, Ted Ray, and Harry Vardon, who among them won 17 British Opens and two U.S. Opens. Braid, Taylor, and Vardon were known as the Great Triumvirate.

they pick up a little more, and an extra shilling or two comes into their pockets from bets. . . . They often sell with great advantage clubs to young players, who fondly imagine magical properties to dwell in the wand itself, rather than in the hands of the sorcerers who wield it. Occasionally they combine with golf-playing more general branches of industry, which they pursue in a spasmodic fashion. Thus, when we asked of one of them whether a brother professional had no other trade than that of golf, he replied, 'Ou, aye! he has that—he breaks stanes.'

"Improvidence in the hours of plenty often brings him to very sore straits. But now that so many more openings are occurring for green-keepers, in the increase in the number of links all over England, we may hope to see these further inducements developing better habits in the professional class."

As we can see from Hutchinson's remarks, the respected and responsible job was that of green-keeper. Yet within a space of fifty years, and in a period when the rigid stratification of society was notably stable, the golf professional evolved to a position of respect and affection. By modern standards he was still, for the most part, a paid retainer of the club and far from achieving equal standing with the members. However, the relationship had changed greatly. His station in life was now more like that of a sergeant major vis-à-vis the officers, or of a head gamekeeper on a large estate. He was a man from whom a gentleman could properly seek advice and tuition. He was the master of his shop and a skilled craftsman. He made and repaired clubs, taught members the techniques of the game, and was much in demand to join them for a round—of golf, that is, not drinks. After the match the pro retired to his shop while the members repaired to the club bar and no one thought anything amiss in that arrangement, least of all the professional himself, who seems to have been content with his lot. Some of today's professionals remember these "good old days,"

regret their passing, and rather resent the emancipation of the profession, since it places on them the burdens of competing socially as well as athletically.

For many of today's senior golfers the professional's shop was where it all began. In those days of hickory-shafted clubs, the shop was a magical place, smelling of tallow, tanned twine, and varnish. In the middle of the clutter was the pro, usually an amiable Scot in tweed plus fours, who made and mended the wonderful adult toys. A boy, if he was lucky, might be privileged to help the great man with small jobs.

Boys, who are great ones for breaking things, have a special respect for people who are skilled at repairs and there is something in youth's nature which associates manual skills with wisdom. The pro was therefore a great man, indeed. In fact, many of them were remarkable men by any standards. Educationalists insist that team games are great character builders. Life, however, is not a team game and to that extent a better case might be made for golf. It teaches a boy self-control, independence, the value of perseverance, and humility. And since golf is a game at which it is so easy to cheat, and so pointless to do so, it places a high premium on honesty. It is a matter of common experience that the golf professional is nearly always a man of sterling character. There are remarkably few bad hats in golf and in this respect those of us who play the game are fortunate.

A few professionals in early times supplemented their club incomes with competitive golf. Pro golf got away to a modest start; formal tournaments were modest in size and numbers. There were only eight entrants for the first Open. Competition golf mainly took the form of challenge matches, and exciting affairs they were, all the more tense for the fact that the golfers were playing for their own money. Willie Park of Musselburgh, a tidy golfer who did not hit the ball very far but was a demon putter, had a standing challenge in the golfing press to play any man for £50 a side, winner take all, and frequently the stakes (worth something like twenty times that today) were higher. Park's motto, "the man who can putt is a match for anyone," was disproved in a famous series of matches with Vardon, but on balance he did well enough.

These challenge matches created enormous public interest and did much to popularize golf, although they brought little direct benefit to the profession. Money circulated, but little was put into the game from outside sources. Cheap golf thus became traditional in Britain, and especially in Scotland. As the national game—or one of them; Scots play every game they adopt with religious fervor—golf was regarded as something of a birthright. Many courses in Scotland, including St. Andrews itself, are owned by the local authorities and golf is provided as a municipal amenity, like water. As a result, even today, the cost of playing a round on a Scottish championship course is less than any self-respecting American visitor would tip his caddie. This accounts for the high proportion of Scottish boys and girls who become very good players at an early age, and it has also resulted in golf being a classless game in Scotland. Much the same situation exists in Ireland.

The historical importance of inexpensive golf in Scotland is that it produced a large number of players of professional standard and skilled clubmakers who could not earn a living in their own country. When golf became the rage in America, there existed a pool of experienced professionals all too anxious to emigrate to the new world. The small village of Carnoustie, which even today is barely more than a one-street town, sent more than a hundred professionals to America to spread the word of golf and put the game on a secure footing.

One such emigrant was given a typically Scottish send-off before departing for South America. He made his farewells and staggered into the night.

When he awoke at dawn from the stupor into which he had fallen, he decided that the first thing he must do was to build a home in this new country. Bemused, he picked out a site before he realized where he was. That hole on the Carnoustie links is known as South America to this day. The story had a happy ending. The emigrant actually built his South American home and lived there for the rest of his life.

While the public has benefited enormously from Scotland's tradition of inexpensive golf, in one respect Scotland has suffered. It is a matter of keen national disappointment that no home-based player has won the Open since the days when the championship was a modest, virtually local competition. Scots *have* won it. Braid took the title five times, but only after he had settled in England. Tommy Armour won the Open in 1931, but by that time he was a naturalized American. Sandy Herd's triumph was muted in his native Scotland by the fact that he had gone to live and work in England.

For some reason which is seated deep within the patriotic breast, there is a special Scotch prejudice against Scots who settle in England. They are known contemptuously as "Anglos." There is a considerable body of Scottish opinion which holds that those guilty of such an act of betrayal as to move to a country where they can earn a living should not be eligible to represent Scotland on international teams.

Can it be that this atavistic prejudice contributes to the phenomenon that, while Scotland produces a large number of very good young players, they do not develop to world class? It may be that the subconscious knowledge that he will almost certainly have to go "abroad" to earn a livelihood, and so attract the odium of the Anglo label, is a disincentive to the young Scottish professional. It is, in other words, more important for him to be true to Scotland than to his own potential. Better a second-grade golfer and a first-class Scot than the other way around.

169

7 · superstars

9 olf's modern era began in 1929, with the perfecting of the tubular steel shaft. As far as playing the game was concerned, it simplified matters considerably, since the golfer no longer had to contend with the problem of torque (the twisting of the shaft during the swing), which made hickory-shafted golf such an exercise in manual control. Straight-grained hickory shafts had many qualities suited to golf. They were strong, flexible, could be shaved to achieve perfect balance, and imparted a lively "feel" to the shot which has never been satisfactorily reproduced by steel, aluminum, or—though it comes close—fiberglass.

The disadvantage of hickory was that it had insufficient resistance to twisting. Under the forces exerted in the golf swing, with the clubhead acting as a lever, this torque action could twist the face "open" at impact. The trick of hickory golf was to time the shot so that the moment of striking coincided with the face in the square position. It was this need for control and timing which made the swings of Vardon and Jones so smooth and graceful. For a player with a short backswing and a powerful action, such as Doug Sanders, hickory golf would be a frustrating activity, since the clubface would always be twisting open at impact. The tubular form of the steel shaft almost eliminated torque and permitted the introduction of hitting at the ball, rather than swinging. Timing still was vital, but now the criterion was to achieve impact at the fastest point in the stroke, with the hands controlling the squareness of the clubface, rather than waiting for the clubhead to square itself, which was the hickory player's problem.

Some golfers made the transition more easily than others. Jones never hit the ball with his old mastery once he took to steel, although it should be remembered that he had long since retired from competitive play. No doubt if he had still been fired by his early spirit and applied his great intellect and golfmanship seriously to the problem, he would quickly have discovered the tricks of the new technique. Some players went on using much hand action in their swings and are remembered for virtuoso shotmaking.

As a generalization, however, the steel shaft and the graduated matched set of irons robbed the game of much of its artistry. The need to contrive different shots for different situations largely disappeared. Today's professionals are much more concerned with using one standard stroke for each of their great variety of clubs. The old school carried many fewer clubs and varied the stroke. If you asked Vardon how far he hit his mashie you received a very dusty answer. It depended entirely on how he played it. Ask Jack Nicklaus the same question about his five-iron and he will tell you to within three yards. It is dangerous to be too dogmatic on this subject because it is not a matter of absolutes. Some modern players do vary their strokes considerably according to conditions. Lee Trevino comes to mind as an example. But, generally, hickory golf was a game of manipulation and inspiration; steel golf is a game of precision and calculation.

With the coming of steel, although not necessarily because of it, golf became a truly international sport. America continued to dominate the game, but other countries, notably Australia and South Africa, began to produce players of world stature. Possibly the most significant figure in this period of transition was Walter Hagen. This brash young man with the patent-leather hair style and flamboyant clothes began his golfing career as a figure of fun. The older pros, brought up in the dour Scottish tradition, did not have much time for this flashy braggart, who announced that he was going to annihilate them and then attempted to make good his boasts with the wildest swing they'd ever seen. However, there was more to Hagen than mouth. He worked hard and, although he never eliminated the exciting possibility of a really dreadful shot, he hit more brilliant ones than anyone else. The brash-

Preceding pages: The greatest? Certainly the most effective golfer of all time with his combination of power, accuracy, competitive spirit, and golfing sense—Jack Nicklaus, here playing in the 1972 Jackie Gleason tournament.

ness matured into confidence in his own superior ability and pretty soon he was cleaning up on the American tournament scene.

Hagen was shrewd enough to understand that the galleries liked their heroes larger than life, and so he stressed his natural tendencies. The clothes became flashier, the bold shots were stage-managed with much pacing about and changing of clubs to make them appear more difficult, and the locker-room psychological warfare ("Who's going to be second?") was ruthlessly continued. Off course, he lived like a millionaire playboy, and a heavily publicized one at that. In comparison with his brother professionals, brought up in the virtues of modesty and self-effacement, Hagen seemed a prince. By behaving as if he could not be beaten, Hagen eventually reached the stage where his opponents began to half-believe he was invincible. The Hagen legend was probably worth two strokes a round to him and each success made the next one that much easier. Of course, Hagen cashed in. That, after all, was the point of the exercise. He toured the world, playing tournaments and challenge matches and giving exhibitions, often in the company of Joe Kirkwood, the trick-shot artist.

What, you may ask, was the significance of a traveling showman who financed his high living with displays of golfing skill? The answer is indirect. Hagen set an example for his brother professionals, an extravagant one, perhaps, but in his style Hagen showed them the possibilities of professional golf. In Britain, for example, the pros were changing their clothes in the caddie sheds and touching their caps to the members—while Hagen hobnobbed with the Prince of Wales, danced until all hours at fashionable night spots, and mixed easily in high society. It did not concern him that as a professional he was not allowed into the clubhouse. His clubhouse was the best hotel in town, far beyond the means of most of the members, and he walked directly to the first tee from the most opulent limousine in the car park. And because he was Hagen, the great champion, the public accepted him as an original character and loved him for it.

In a rather different category at this time was Henry Cotton, a dedicated and remote English pro. Cotton did not conform either. He was, for a start, a gentleman and had been educated at a good public school. Unlike Hagen, Cotton knew the social rules and knew all too well that by becoming a pro he was déclassé. Cotton refused to play the conventions of that snobbish game. He, too, stayed at the Ritz and his chauffeur-driven Rolls-Royce was his clubhouse. While the pros went off to the caddie shed to eat their cheese sandwiches and the members repaired to the club for Lancashire hot pot, Cotton had his man produce a Fortnum & Mason hamper from the Rolls and picnicked on caviar and champagne. The popping of the cork was largely symbolic, for the highly strung Cotton could take only the lightest refreshment during the tension of a tournament, but it sounded the opening shot of a social revolution.

The barriers of social prejudice could not withstand such an elegant assault. Between them, Hagen and Cotton opened the clubhouse doors and gradually the golf professional was accepted on terms of equality by the members.

In the United States, where it is not a crime to be born poor provided you do not stay that way, the period following the retirement of Jones brought two golfers to full maturity. It is true that a young Italian felt it prudent to Anglicize his name from Saraceni to Sarazen, but thereafter his only obstacles were the regular hazards of any golfing career.

Gene Sarazen brought more to golf than an outstanding gift for the game. Blessed with a lively and progressive intellect he advanced the techniques of golf in one notable manner. At this time the all-purpose club for high pitches around the green and for bunker play was the broad-faced niblick. This club, with its thin, almost circular face, had a cutting edge like an ax, and in the hands of a skilled player was a spectacular instrument. A player could open the face and cut up the ball with an almost vertical trajectory to clear an obstacle, or hood the face and hit a low, punched shot into the wind. While it was a most versatile club when the shot succeeded, it had vast potential for disaster. Unless the stroke was perfectly executed the result could be damaging. Hit the ball a fraction thin and that sharp cutting edge sent it skimming yards past the target—and probably cut the cover in the bargain. Hit the shot fat and the clubface dug into the turf and resulted in the feeblest of duffs. In bunkers, where the technique was to skim the blade under the ball, an error either way left the ball in the sand.

Sarazen felt that this club was altogether too chancy. In the tension of tournament golf a club was needed which could be relied upon to get the ball out of sand every time, even if the execution was not perfect. He experimented by welding a flange onto the bottom of the club, shaping it in such a way that when he hit down with it, the clubhead did not dig farther into the sand but was instead deflected upward. So the family of wedges was started, later evolving into specialized clubs for sand and pitching purposes. Players such as Billy Casper and Gary Player have achieved such mastery of the wedges that it is unthinkable they could do better with any other form of club.

Yet in one way it is a pity that Sarazen's new club enjoyed such success, for it tended to discredit the old spade niblick entirely. Certainly the wedge is more reliable and gives the player a welcome margin for error. But there are some things the wedge cannot do, even in the hands of a master, which are possible with the niblick. All of us have been faced at times with a fluffy lie on a downslope with the prospect of having to carry a bunker and trying to stop the ball quickly on a fast and sloping green. In this situation the pro lays open his sand wedge and tries to play a delicate, lazy-looking shot. But that flange, so useful in sand, is now a hindrance and unless the stroke is perfect the clubhead may bounce into the ball and ruin the shot. The thin-bladed niblick could be skimmed smartly under the ball, which popped into the air, floated down to the green, landed softly as a cat, and braked hard with backspin. Such a club does not fit the so-called "matched" set. It would appear to be an odd-man out. All the same, there is a good case for its revival—just as there is for the jigger, the useful club for short run-ups. Certainly our stereotyped attitude toward clubs could profitably be reexamined.

Along with Sarazen, we must consider the career of Byron Nelson, or at any rate one season in that career. In 1945 Nelson, a quiet Texan, won eighteen official PGA tournaments, eleven of them in succession. His season's stroke average was 68.33. They say that nobody remembers who came second, but it is worth a footnote to Nelson's year that he finished as runner-up seven times, and that his worst performance of the season was ninth. His winnings, incidentally, amounted to $52,500, and it is possibly worth remarking that if anyone could reproduce that record today he would win rather more than $700,000.

Some people have argued, rather ungenerously, that since this was wartime Nelson did not have much opposition. Perhaps there were not many great players among the opposition, although with Ben Hogan and Sam Snead in the line-up, no tournament was a pushover. Nelson's real achievement, however, was not the winning but the manner of winning. A stroke average of 68.33 brooks no argument. For consistency there has never been anything like it, before or since. This was the only year Nelson devoted fully to tournament play. Until then he had been mainly a club pro, and afterward, having won the U.S. Open, Masters, and PGA championships, and with his ambitions sated by records, he eased into semiretirement.

There have been many judgments of Nel-

Gene Sarazen (l.), in one sense the first of
the modern breed of professional. He brought a lively
intelligence and deeply analytical approach to
the game and pioneered the use of broad-soled wedges.

Golf's first showman, the dandy Walter Hagen, who talked a great game of golf and who most of the time matched his words with his deeds on the course. Opposite: With Californian star Helen Lawson.

son's golf by his contemporaries, and the consensus is that during 1945, when he played almost as if in a trance, his iron play, in particular the confidence with which he worked and finessed the ball up to the flag, was his greatest strength. A dissenting minority holds the view that his supremacy lay in his driving. He always hit his approach shots from the right place and was naturally more successful with them than his rivals. The evidence of Nelson himself can be called to support both sides. Nelson rather dismisses his driving, modestly conceding only that it was very consistent at that time. This may be taken to mean he felt his approach work was the more telling part of his game. On the other hand, it also could mean that he paid little attention to it because he did not need to, and therefore took it for granted. His retirement, prompted no doubt by a temperament which did not relish the nervous tensions of tournament golf, cut off a career which might have reached any heights. As it was, he packed into that one year enough successes to sustain most players for twenty years or more.

The idea has grown that Nelson's year of triumph was a phenomenon which defies explanation. He himself has given some weight to that theory by admitting to being superstitious and saying that perhaps this period was a particularly propitious one for him. Every golfer has at times enjoyed the experience of knowing with utter certainty that the long putt he is about to strike is going to fall into the cup. Such moments of enlightenment occasionally accompany other types of shots. In Nelson's case, there is another and more prosaic factor. Before that season began he carefully analyzed the weaknesses in his game. He objectively researched the areas of his golf where strokes could be saved and made a number of adjustments to his play, such as altering his technique for short chip shots. He also made a slight but fundamental change in his swing, getting into a more upright plane with his feet positioned closer to the ball.

This upright style, sometimes glibly called the American swing, may have been the key to his successes. Every individual has what may be called an optimum arc, a swing plane which suits him best. It is obviously a personal trait, which is why the search for the perfect, "universal" swing is such a forlorn cause. Lee Trevino clearly performs best with a flat, sweeping swing, while Jack Nicklaus is better with an upright style. The trouble with most of us golfers is that we try to model ourselves on (or allow ourselves to be taught) styles which may not be suitable to our personal idiosyncrasies. Perhaps Byron Nelson found his best swing plane in the spring of 1945 and the rest just followed naturally.

So-called style, or good form, has bedeviled modern golf and we do not have to look far for the culprit. Ben Hogan, the singleminded perfectionist, made himself into the finest striker of a golf ball the world has ever known. He came nearer than anyone to perfecting golf. Unwittingly he became the model for millions of golfers who argued with simple logic that since Hogan's results were best, Hogan's methods must be best. So they were—for Hogan. And that's where the logic broke down. Manifestly we are not all Hogans, and it is futile to pretend we are. What worked for Hogan may be absurd for a short, fat executive of advancing years whose muscles are conditioned for the chairbound life. When we see someone like the 6-foot 5-inch George Archer play golf we are not surprised that his swing is not like Hogan's. Obviously it could not be. What is less obvious, but equally true, is that the golfer who is an exact physical match for Hogan in his prime may be totally unsuited to Hogan's method of swinging a golf club. There is much in Hogan's golf and life, of course, which the aspiring young golfer can usefully copy. His dedication, his perseverance, and his courage are models for all. But as to method, the young player would be wise to follow Hogan only as far as the great man's own start-

The typical Haig—cool, calm, and collecting
British Open trophy in Sandwich, 1928, while his golfing friend,
Edward, Prince of Wales, listens deferentially
behind him. After all, on the course Hagen was King.

ing point—and that is to go out and discover by long experiment and painstaking practice what works best for him. What he has to develop is a swing that delivers the clubhead to the ball at speed, square to the line of flight, along the line of flight, and at the appropriate angle of attack (that is to say, not scooping or digging). Any eccentricity of swing is permissible provided that the four·golden rules of impact are consistently achieved. The trouble with unorthodox methods is that, while they work well for a time, they often put such physical strains on a golfer that his swing does not endure. The method that works for most people is the so-called classical style exemplified by the swing of

Sam Snead and which has served him for more than forty years.

It is interesting to observe the new generation of young professionals and try to isolate common points of style which might then be defined as "the modern swing." There is only one common denominator and even that is not entirely universal. It arises from the basic difference between pro and amateur golf. The amateur wants to score as low as possible while the pro is concerned not to produce a high score. It is, of course, a matter of emphasis rather than dogma, but the difference is there.

In the last analysis it does not matter if

*Two international stars—Henry Cotton
of England, three times Open champion, and (opposite on
right) South Africa's Bobby Locke, who won five
Opens and was probably finest putter in history of golf.*

an amateur takes an 80. All he hurts is his ego. But for the pro, an 80 can mean that he does not eat that week. If he can average par for a season he will live well; indeed, in some years such an average would make him the leading moneywinner. As a result, his thinking about the golf swing is directed toward the elimination of error. Control is everything. Most amateurs—and the old-time pros as well—play with a loosely hinging wrist action at the top of the backswing. It is a powerful technique, since the clubhead describes a full arc, but it requires immaculate timing to deliver the clubface to the ball in exactly the right place at exactly the maximum clubhead speed. In the new golf as played by the pros, such an action is characterized as "floppy at the top," and they work to achieve a controlled firmness of the wrists at the top of the backswing. Of course, if they left it at that their arcs would be shortened and they would lose distance. So they work—and it really is work in the sense of physical athleticism—to increase the body turn. They coil the spring that much tighter.

If an amateur golfer is interested in reducing his handicap there is much he can learn by watching, say, Jack Nicklaus, provided he is prepared to be honest with himself. Imagine a typical situation. A 15-handicap player watching television sees Nicklaus, in knee-high rough, take out his seven-iron and smash the ball onto a green 180 yards away. The commentator explodes with ecstasy, as if this were a miracle rather than an everyday occurrence. Then a slow-motion replay is shown with an expert pointing out, "Notice the way Jack keeps his head absolutely still during the stroke." If our 15-handicap friend tries to emulate Nicklaus in that situation he is headed straight for the osteopath's couch and bitter disillusionment. But there is a useful lesson to be learned, provided the amateur is prepared to deal in realities rather than fantasy. The question the amateur golfer must ask himself is: "What would Nicklaus do now, *if*

he had a swing like mine?"

Now we can pick Nicklaus's golfing brain. Now the amateur, if he has been watching sensibly, has Nicklaus at his side nominating the shot. And the answer is obvious: Take a wedge, pick a spot on the fairway, and very deliberately pitch the ball out sideways to the safety of the mown surface. Then you can play an ordinary approach. Sure, you may drop a shot. But at worst you are home with a 5 instead of a certain 8. And, who knows, you might sink a putt and save your par. Even with all his skill, Nicklaus seldom aims directly at the flag. He plays the percentages and goes for the center of the green. And he is Jack Nicklaus. Where do you get off, with your 15-handicap swing, firing away at the pin? The one important lesson the club golfer can learn from watching the pros is to play within the limits of his ability. The pro goes for the shot he knows he can produce. All too often the amateur gambles on what he recognizes (if he stops to think about it) must be the shot of a lifetime for him.

Hogan's distinguished record did not adequately reflect the clear superiority of his golf. This is partly explained by the loss of what should have been some of his most productive years, and partly by the premature onset of putting troubles. As is well known, Hogan suffered multiple fractures when he threw himself across his wife to save her as their car smashed into a bus. That seemed to end the most polished golfing talent the world had ever seen, but Hogan confounded his doctors by torturing his broken body back to golfing fitness, and claiming once more his place at the peak of American golf. Anyone, however, who plays golf with the intensity of a Hogan, a man to whom every shot was a matter of vital importance, must be liable sooner or later to what we callously call the yips, or twitch. This is a nervous complaint or, more accurately, a symptom of a nervous condition. Its effect is to short-circuit the lines of communication between the brain and the hands, thus bringing about a break-

Postwar swingers. Standing (l. to r.): Henry Picard, Martin Pose, Jimmy Hines, Horton Smith, Gene Sarazen, Lawson Little, Jimmy Thomson, Sam Snead; front: Ben Hogan, Byron Nelson, Jimmy Demaret, Dick Metz, Craig Wood, Paul Runyan, Clayton Heafner.

down in free will. The brain commands the hands to take the putter back slowly, but there is no response. Eventually the message gets through in the form of a desperate SOS and the hands respond with an uncontrolled jerk. The yips are caused by tension, and it is only in the heat of a tournament that they occur.

Sufferers will try anything to cure this condition, but changing grips or putters, or trying to exorcise the spell on the practice green, is useless. The one possible way to a cure is to induce a relaxed frame of mind, but since golfers may spend twenty years on the circuit without conquering their nervous tension, this is easier said than done.

The only practical palliative is for the golfer to immobilize the affected muscles. Usually the yips start with the smaller muscles of the fingers, those normally employed for delicate work. In that case, control can be regained—albeit at the expense of some degree of touch—by locking the hands on the club and putting with an arm action. If the arms are also affected they can be locked, clamped firmly against the side, and the putter moved by a swaying motion of the hips. This may not be a particularly effective method of holing out, but at least it gives the twitcher a chance to regain a measure of confidence.

It is one thing to tell an ordinary club golfer with the yips that salvation lies in taking his golf, and perhaps himself, less seriously. But such a cure was not open to Hogan. At his level golf is serious by definition. Unless the player gives the game total concentration it loses its point. Hence, one of the saddest sights in modern golf was the last competitive appearances of Ben Hogan. The command with which he struck the ball from tee to green was nullified by his sweating agony as he stood locked over a putt. Eventually, by a huge effort of will, he broke the paralysis

with a convulsion which might send the ball 20 feet past its target. Those people who urged Hogan to return to big-time golf on the grounds that he still hit the ball better than anyone did not realize the ordeal they were asking him to endure. To Hogan there was no satisfaction in giving what amounted to exhibitions of stroke play. He did not have to prove anything. Golf has always been two games. At one of them Hogan was unrivaled. At the other, the game within a game, he could no longer compete. And since these games cannot be separated, he called it a day.

No one could ever accuse Bobby Locke of being a slave to style or to any golfing orthodoxy. In many ways Locke was the opposite of Hogan. It is impossible to describe his swing without making it sound like a parody, which in truth it was. The American public was astonished at the sight of this young South African, whose naturally cheerful personality was rigorously subdued on the course behind a solemn expression as unchanging as a mask; he had the stately air of an archbishop conducting a funeral. He set himself as if to hit the ball forty-five degrees to the right of the target, and he took the club back with an action which was more of a pirouette than a backswing. From here he swung down and delivered what appeared to be a rather dainty flick at the ball, following through to another pirouette. The ball flew off in the direction you would expect from such an exaggeratedly closed stance and many were the suppressed smiles as Old Muffin Face's ball flew toward the right-hand rough.

Then, in keeping with his ecclesiastical demeanor, the miracle occurred. As the ball reached the height of its trajectory, it went into a left turn and homed back to the fairway. Every shot was the same controlled draw. Even the short irons started out right of the flag and, as if under remote-control guidance,

Three women champions—Glenna Collett Vare, national champion six times; Patty Berg, national and Open champion; and one of the greatest sportswomen America (or anywhere else) has produced—Babe Didrikson Zaharias.

plummeted back on target. If the galleries found Locke's highly personal method amusing, there was very little laughter among his fellow professionals. This guy was picking up fat checks week after week and taking the bread out of their mouths.

Locke's right-to-left style was not suited to all conditions and courses. Most modern professionals prefer to move the ball the other way, with a slight fade. The higher trajectory of the fade and increased braking effect on landing give the golfer greater control, since his shots are less likely to run on into trouble. Locke, however, had two other assets. From tee to green his philosophy was unadventurous in the extreme. He played well within himself and his drive nearly always finished twenty yards short of his fellow competitor's ball (although he could belt it out with the best of them when he wanted). Most of the time he was content simply to move the ball modestly or safely forward. But once on the green he had a decided edge because he was by general consent the finest putter of his day.

He had an unvarying routine with an old hickory-shafted blade putter. This began with a close examination of the line, even down to what appeared to be a distasteful examination of the hole itself, like a head waiter examining a bowl of soup which has been the subject of a complaint. People used to joke that Locke was reassuring himself that the hole was big enough to receive his ball, but the explanation was less fanciful. Brought up on the nappy greens of South Africa, he had naturally fallen into the habit of inspecting the rim of the cup to confirm the direction of the nap. And Locke was nothing if not a creature of habit. After this leisurely reconnaissance he became decidedly brisk. He took his stance, made two quick practice putts, shuffled an inch or so forward, and hit the putt with a rhythmic, wristy stroke which found the cup in an astonishingly high proportion of cases.

But hit or miss, his deadpan expression never changed and here was Locke's second great asset. Temperamentally and emotionally the man was fireproof, or so it seemed. He suffered from nervous tension of course. Everyone does. But by self-discipline he trained himself never to show by the flicker of an eyebrow how he was feeling. Just how much this self-control helped him to suppress his natural jitters we do not know, but what is beyond dispute is that by seeming never to lose his cool, the other players believed him to be nerveless. And that in itself, as in the case of Walter Hagen, was a considerable advantage to Locke.

Locke was the first major figure to be produced by what we might call the emergent golfing nations. The breach in Anglo-American domination of the game was quickly widened by more great players from different nations. Along came Roberto de Vicenzo of Argentina, a superb striker and proof that this serious new game need not be solemn or lose its qualities as a sport, despite the arrival of the businessman pro. Peter Thomson of Australia has never received his due recognition as a player and influential administrator, either in America or, strangely enough, in his own country. Yet his contribution to the advancement of golf and the improvement in conditions of the profession, not to mention his contribution to the record books, is unsurpassed. His reputation in America suffered because he is an uncompromising enthusiast for old-fashioned natural golf. He believes that golf should remain a game of inspiration, unraked bunkers, and improvised shot-making. He even approves of the element of chance, the lucky or unlucky bounce, and so it is perhaps natural that his views were received coolly in a country where the tendency is to take luck out of golf as much as possible. However, his lack of recognition in Australia is less easy to understand, especially as sport in his country is almost a national religion.

New Zealand has produced Bob Charles, the only left-hander to achieve international status. That fact is difficult to explain in the light of the pro-

The agony and the payoff for Gary Player,
the small South African whose dedication elevated him to
the front ranks of the golfing giants. Bottom:
With his wife after another of his championship triumphs.

portion of lefties occurring in nature. If golf is compared with, say, tennis, the dearth of left-handers is astonishing and the only explanation is that young golfers are encouraged to play the wrong way round. A left-handed boy is advised to persevere with right-handed clubs on the grounds that in golf the left hand should dominate the swing. This doctrine that golf is a left-handed game, which can easily be proved false, must have done incomparable harm to many thousands of players who would have been better and happier as southpaws.

In the sixties, golf became a truly international game. Nothing proved this more completely than the emergence of the so-called Big Three (echoes of the Great Triumvirate) in the person of two Americans, Arnold Palmer and Jack Nicklaus, and a South African, Gary Player. If their manager, Mark McCormack, had

sat down and worked out the theoretical specifications for a national sporting idol he would have come up with a blueprint for an Arnold Palmer. Appearance: rough-hewn good looks and the air of a boy who is up to devilment; a face that is quick to smile and which clearly reflects its owner's moods. Physical assets: the build of a good middleweight; big hands; long, tapering back; strong, stocky legs—the perfect conformation for hitting a golf ball. Personality: tough, aggressive, and self-centered, but with an easy-going and responsive veneer and a taste for the dramatic. It is little wonder that once Palmer began to win he attracted a huge personal following, both for his golf and his personality.

Palmer's swing is no classic. On the backswing he tends to throw the club out of its plane, so that coming down he has to fight to bring the clubhead

Admiration and elation: Popular Charles Sifford,
whose dexterity with a golf club is matched only by his
skill at cigar chomping, and (opposite) Billy Casper
hailing one that dropped for him in the 1971 PGA Championship.

*Gallery favorites: Lee Trevino signs, Ben Hogan
swings, and Sam Snead does his unorthodox
thing on the green. His sidewinder putting works—for him.
Right: Palmer, Nicklaus, and Trevino at World Series.*

190

into the "slot." This compensating action gives him his characteristic high finish with a "twiddly bit" at the end, and when his timing is slightly off, as it must be with everyone at times, his bad shots are likely to be wilder than the mis-hits of more conventional swingers. However, Palmer's greatest asset is a combination of a gambling instinct (or optimism or foolhardiness) which makes him attempt dramatic recoveries from trouble, and his physical strength, which so frequently makes these attempts successful.

The ordinary spectator cannot relate to a Ben Hogan, because his brand of flawless golf is entirely outside the ordinary run of country-club golf. Not so Palmer. He gets himself into places which are all too familiar to the Sunday morning four-ball. The difference is that Palmer extricates himself with his score unscathed. The spectator can admire Hogan in a cool, objective sense, but he can bleed with Palmer and rejoice with him at the happy ending. If Harry Vardon changed the method of golf, Palmer more than any man changed the manner of the game. His deeds on the course turned golf into a major spectator sport and a multimillion-dollar business.

The case of Gary Player was quite different. As a youth he would not have fitted anyone's blueprint for a sporting hero. He was small and frail, and his golf, both in the way he gripped the club and the way he swung it, suggested he would be better advised to take up a different career. But circumstances of background and physique combined to produce in

Player a classic Napoleon complex. He believed in Gary Player. And with the thoroughness of a true fanatic he set out methodically to prove the adage of the song that "anything you can do I can do better." If he was too small and weak, he would make himself big and strong. If his grip and swing were unsound, he would change them and make them the best in the business. Player's campaign of self-improvement was the most punishing body-building regime any golfer has ever undertaken. He practiced longer than anyone else. He favored diets of nuts and fresh fruits. The zeal which he lavished on his body reached cranky proportions. At one time he wore black outfits "to absorb the strength of the sun," and he pursued every health fad on the market. And he did not neglect his mind. Those around him may have thought his attitude of "my strength is as the strength of ten because my heart is pure" was sanctimonious, but in total the mystical amalgam of nuts, fingertip pushups, and divine inspiration has worked.

He became a great golfer, as good as anyone around, and pound for pound better than any of them. In the process, the overcoming of handicaps became habit-forming. As a major figure in world golf, with nothing left to prove, Player still has to prove himself to himself every time he plays. With no obstacles to overcome he must invent imaginary ones. Hence, his outbursts against the condition of courses, or the "hook" which he claims is plaguing his game. If he can raise a demon for his combative spirit to wrestle and overthrow, he is a magnificent golfer. Have him 7 down against Tony Lema with 18 holes to play in the Piccadilly match-play tournament, and he produces the most remarkable golf of his career. It is not enough for Player to beat his colleagues. If the whole world is against him, as it seemed to him in the beginning, then Player has an opponent worthy of his mettle.

Jack Nicklaus, too, faced more than the golfer's traditional enemy, par, when he came into the pro game. He had to fight a legend. Nicklaus, a prodigy as a young amateur who had almost snatched the U.S. Open championship from the cream of professional golf, was always going to be one of the greats. Nobody doubted that fact for a moment after watching the big teen-ager belt out a drive. The trouble was that there can only be one rooster on top of the haystack and that perch belonged to Palmer. If Nicklaus was to become champion he would have to depose the darling of the golf world.

That did not worry the two golfers unduly. Such, after all, is the way of sport. But for the hero-worshipping public Nicklaus was the iconoclast who threatened to smash their idol. At that time Nicklaus thought of nothing but golf. Issues such as personal appearance and public relations did not help him hit a golf ball and so were no concern to him. In time he grew to appreciate that they did, indeed, affect both his golf and his income, but as a youngster subtleties of this kind entirely escaped him. He was frankly fat and his crew-cut hair accentuated a quality that people quickly associated with arrogance. In fact, Nicklaus has his share of the arrogance essential to a champion, but in his case it is more an honest realization of his capabilities. In the British Open of 1971, against Doug Sanders, when Nicklaus peeled off his sweater and drove through the last green 385 yards away, it looked like an act of arrogance. In reality, it was an example of his rather conservative nature. He was playing safe. He knew objectively that in those conditions he could have reached his target with a three-wood, but he cautiously took his driver to make sure.

In the same way his deeds and public utterances were often misconstrued when he first became a professional, especially at that time when many people were all too eager to see him in a bad light. The Palmer-oriented galleries booed him shamelessly and nothing that Nicklaus has achieved in golf is more becoming than his dignified behavior during that trying period of his career. If he suffered privately he kept it to himself and gradually his golf won him due respect. In fact, the booing was probably counterproductive in total effect, because although it may have upset Nicklaus it certainly embarrassed Palmer and probably upset him more.

What makes Nicklaus the greatest golfer of his generation? He does not strike the ball with anything like the consistency of Hogan. His short game and putting are probably below the standard of the average tournament professional, and his golfing outlook is possibly too conservative. The answer, of course, is power, but it would be a gross oversimplification to see Nicklaus as just a slugger. Many of his triumphs, after all, have been achieved on short courses where there is no great premium on length. The key to his success is power through the full range of clubs. It is obvious, except in the case of oddities like Britain's Tommy Horton, that a golfer is more accurate with an eight-iron than he is with a four. If we categorize the long irons, one to four, as being mainly distance clubs and the others, five to nine, as predominately accuracy clubs, then we can see that Nicklaus is often playing for accuracy while his opponents are more concerned with distance. He may take a one-iron off the tee and seemingly throw away the advantage of his power. But then, when he and his opponent are both roughly in the same part of the fairway, Nicklaus can hit a six-iron while the rest need fours. And if the circumstances are propitious, as on that day at St. Andrews, he can let out his driver and give himself an even greater advantage with his second shot.

There are, it is true, some golfers who can hit the ball as far as Nicklaus, club for club, but they are the true sluggers who hit flat out. Nicklaus gets his distance while playing well within his physical powers and he therefore has the edge in accuracy. In the record books Nicklaus has already proved himself the most formidable player of all. (He cannot be compared with Bobby Jones because of the vast difference in their circumstances. No matter how many championships Nicklaus wins he can never usurp Jones' standing as the greatest of them all. Better, yes, but greatness involves more than scoring and the manner of Jones' triumphs cannot be approached.)

If we are mainly concerned with significant contributions to golf the superficial view of Nicklaus is as the first of the great method players. He pioneered the system of pacing out courses and charting distance. However, that is a mere matter of mathematics, and the natural product of his logical mind. Indeed, many people would argue that the habit of measuring every shot diminished golf in that it robbed the game of an element of judgment and, perhaps more important, added a time-consuming ritual to a game which had already become intolerably slow. Since it is inevitable that club players will copy the acknowledged masters of the game, pacing and other tedious pro habits have become a commonplace (and pointless) exercise for lesser golfers, and a round of four-ball play has come to mean a five-hour marathon (instead of the old norm, about three and a quarter hours).

No, we can hardly heap laurels on Nicklaus for his part in this retrograde tendency. His contribution is more like that of Harry Vardon in setting a new standard of play. It is almost a cliché among tournament players to pass remarks to the effect, "When Jack is on form the rest of us are playing for second place." They cannot hope to live with him at his best. However, the younger players coming into the game are not daunted by Nicklaus, simply because it is the nature of youthful ambition to set no limits to their potential. For them Nicklaus represents the standard which they must attain and surpass. Just as Roger Bannister's four-minute mile released a psychological block in athletics and ushered in an era of unprecedented speed, so the standards of Nicklaus have opened the way for a generation of super-golfers.

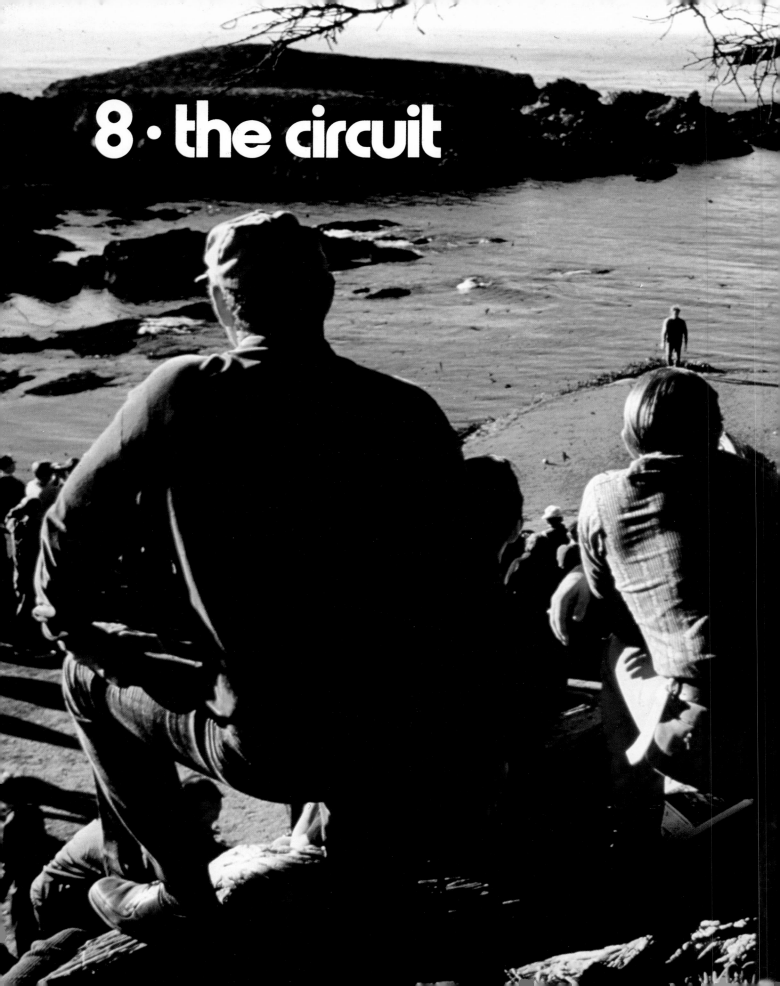

8 · the circuit

much in the manner of the British postage stamp, which has no word to label the country of origin, so in golf it is not the British Open but simply the Open Championship. This is not affectation. When the event began it was the only one, so there was no reason to distinguish it. However, to avoid confusion we will refer to it as the British Open and risk the wrath of pedants.

It all began casually enough when the Prestwick Club was formed. The idea of a general golf tournament was kicked around in committee for several years. At last, in 1860, they got around to playing it, with eight invited players competing for a handsome red morocco belt mounted with silver plaques. They played 36 holes in one day, three rounds of Prestwick's 12-hole links, and it is interesting to recall in the light of today's turgid, five-hour rounds that those first Open contestants did not hit off until after lunch. It was four years before the idea of prize money arose, and even then it was limited to £5 for the runner-up, £3 for third, and £2 for fourth. The tradition that glory was more important than financial reward, which was later to bring the Open into low repute, was thus established from the start.

In the first eight years the original field of eight was augmented by additional players from time to time (they had fourteen entries one year), and the stout figure of Prestwick's home pro, the splendidly bearded Tom Morris, was adorned by the championship belt four times. In 1868 the fans had to start referring to him as Old Tom because his seventeen-year-old son, Young Tom Morris, burst upon the golfing scene and swept the board with an unprecedented score of 154. He won it the next two years in succession and so, according to the rules, the belt became his property. That set a problem for the host club and a year elapsed before it succeeded in finding a satisfactory solution. The outcome was that Prestwick joined forces with St. Andrews and the Honourable Company of Edinburgh Golfers and subscribed for the present cup, on condition that the championship be held at each of the three clubs in turn. Thus the foundation of the modern Open was laid, although at that time it inspired vastly less interest than the club championships. Rather, it was a novelty tournament for the servants of the game. It was not until 1892 that the championship was extended to 72 holes, or four rounds of the standardized 18-hole course.

By now the Open had begun to accumulate a respectable fallout of the anecdote and legend from which tradition is formed. Modern promoters try all manner of tricks to buy instant tradition, but there is no shortcut to the real thing. The golfer who registers for an Open Championship at St. Andrews cannot fail to be affected by the history of the event; a newly sponsored tournament, even though it is over the same course for the same, or bigger, purses cannot provoke the same response.

One of the incidents which helped build the awesome tradition of the Open was the experience of David Ayton at St. Andrews in 1885. Ayton came to the 17th five shots ahead of the field in the last round, and when he hit two good shots to the throat of the green everyone believed it was all over. He ran up his approach shot rather gently—after all, he could afford a conservative 6 if need be—but the ball rolled back down the slope of the green and stopped in front of the bunker. We can now imagine him telling himself that the one thing he must guard against is the ignominy of topping the ball feebly into the sand. He played boldly, a shade too boldly, and the ball rolled over the far brow of the green down onto the road. Four. We do not know how he felt as he addressed that first recovery shot from the road. But when his ball failed to make the green it is a safe bet that the panic of desperation guided his second attempt. He got it up off the road all right—and into a bunker. Having lost two shots on that road he didn't want to return there and

Preceding pages: The most beautiful, and most exasperating, par-3 in the world—240 yards across the bay for the 16th at Cypress Point, California. Bing Crosby had a hole-in-one here.

196

his first bunker shot was indecisive. The ball stayed in the sand. Seven. It was still there after his next sweating attempt. Eight. Out it came on the third try, and two putts gave him an 11. He lost the Open by two strokes and golfers began referring to the 17th as "the dreaded road hole." The legend had begun, spread from golfer to golfer by word of mouth and doubtless embellished in each retelling.

With the rise of the Great Triumvirate of J. H. Taylor, James Braid, and Harry Vardon, the Open became more or less the private preserve of these three around the turn of the century. And, as if it were not painful enough for Scottish pride to have a couple of Englishmen beating them at their own game, the Open was now extended to England on a rota system which brought it to Hoylake, near Liverpool, and Sandwich on the south coast. By modern standards both courses seem hopelessly old-fashioned, and they are now off the Open championships rota because of their inadequate amenities. In many ways it is unfortunate that big golfing events today have to be staged at clubs chosen for such extraneous reasons as parking space rather than golfing excellence. In these cases, however, we need not regret their absence too deeply.

When Harry Vardon won a record sixth Open at Prestwick in 1914, an era came to an end. The war put the Open into abeyance for six years and when it was resumed a new breed of golfer came to the fore, mainly from across the Atlantic. The first was an expatriate Scot, Jock Hutchison, but he was followed by native-born Walter Hagen, Jim Barnes, Gene Sarazen, Denny Shute (also an ex-Scot), Tommy Armour, and the amateur Bobby Jones. Armour was a remarkable character. As an amateur he played for Great Britain's Walker Cup team and then, having been decorated for bravery in the war, he emigrated to America, became a naturalized citizen, and represented the USA in Ryder Cup play. At the end of his distinguished playing career he won a new reputation as a teacher of golf.

These were lean days for the British home professionals, but highly significant ones in the history of golf. As we have seen, Jones completed his Grand Slam and Hagen laid the foundations for modern tournament golf. These two men were responsible for two of the famous single shots in the history of golf, both on the same day. It was the last round of the 1926 Open at Royal Lytham and St. Anne's, and Jones, playing with the leader Al Watrous, started two shots behind. By the 17th they were level, and Watrous hit a good drive up the fairway, leaving him a clear sight of the green on this slightly doglegged hole. Jones, usually the straightest of drivers, for once pulled his tee shot. He not only missed the fairway on the wrong side—he could not even see the green over a wilderness of scrub and bushes—but his ball lay on a sandy scrape. Today the spot is a formal fairway bunker, but in those days it was no more than a barren area of rough sand. Jones took his mashie and played a superb shot, taking the ball cleanly off the top of the sand. It drifted slightly in the crosswind, as Jones had intended, and finished inside Watrous' ball on the green. Watrous, thoroughly unnerved by this master stroke, three-putted and Jones made his 4. The site of that knockout shot is today marked by a commemorative bronze plaque.

Jones, having safely disposed of his main challenger, was in the clubhouse watching the remaining players finish. The only possible threat lay with Hagen, and even that was a million-to-one chance. If Hagen could get down in two on the long par-4 last hole he could tie with Jones. Hagen hit a good drive which left him about 150 yards from the green. He asked his scorer to go forward and hold the flagstick. The official, after an incredulous pause, advanced just short of the green and stopped. Hagen had to walk forward and shout: "I want you to hold the flag." The gallery roared with delight. There are witnesses who swear that if the flag had been left in the hole Hagen's shot would have hit it and possibly dropped in. As it happened the ball pitched dead on line, hopped over the hole and ran through the green. Jones told Hagen later: "I turned my back on you, Walter, because a guy with that much confidence would be fool lucky enough to make it."

Some years later, in 1947, a similar situation arose at Hoylake. The Irishman Fred Daly was in the club not daring to watch as the great American amateur Frank Stranahan came to the last needing a 2 to upset the apple cart. Like Hagen, he hit a fine drive and left himself 150 yards from the green. He walked all the way to the hole before rolling up his sleeves and hitting a perfect shot. The ball pitched dead on line and rolled straight at the flag. With the roar of the crowd rising to a frenzy, the ball died just six inches short of the cup.

It was not until 1934, with the emergence of Henry Cotton, that British golf began to produce a succession of domestic champions. Cynical observers have commented that this period of British domination in the Open coincides with the period of extreme isolationism in America and that the political stay-at-home mood extended to professional golfers. The charge has little substance. Cotton's opening 67 at Sandwich gave him a good lead, and when he followed with a 65, the lowest round in the history of the championship, he had the field at his mercy. The weather turned foul for the third round and Cotton's 72 was good enough to keep him well clear. He had such a lead, in fact, that a severe attack of stomach cramps and a last round of 79 was still good enough for a five-shot victory. Regardless of the opposition, this was irresistible golf.

And three years later no one could criticize the quality of the field over the toughest course on the rota, Carnoustie on the west coast of Scotland. The American Ryder Cup team had just inflicted a crushing defeat on the British and was present in force for the Open. Gene Sarazen and Tony Manero missed the cut, but that still left Walter Hagen, Sam Snead, Byron Nelson, Horton Smith, Ed Dudley, Henry Picard, Denny Shute, Ralph Guldahl, and Johnny Revolta in the shake-up. As if it was not enough that Carnoustie should be intrinsically the most testing championship course, the weather took a hand, as it does so often on Scottish links. The last round was played in a lashing rainstorm. Everyone was soaked to the skin and any possibility of keeping grips dry was out of the question. Cotton always maintained that his 71 in those conditions was the best round of his career.

Another of the celebrated single strokes in the history of the Open was played by Harry Bradshaw at Sandwich in 1950. In retrospect, it now seems clear that the shot should not have been played at all. In the second round Bradshaw pushed his drive into the rough and when he found his ball he saw it lay inside half of a broken beer bottle. Nowadays, of course, any pro in a similar predicament would sit down on his bag and wait for a referee to come and give him his due privilege of dropping the ball clear without penalty. In those days, however, there were no experts on hand to give rulings. The happy-go-lucky Bradshaw, brought up on the principle of playing the ball wherever it might lie, never for a moment considered an alternative. He took his venerable wedge, closed his eyes to protect them from flying glass, and smashed at the bottle. The ball moved twenty yards or so. The incident, nevertheless, unnerved him and the strokes he lost on this hole possibly cost him the title. He tied with the South African Bobby Locke and was decisively beaten in the play-off. Many a golfer would carry the scars of such an incident to his grave. Not Bradshaw, who says of it: "I am only proud to have earned a play-off with a grand champion like Bobby Locke."

The event did leave its mark, however.

Here we make a distinction between *golfer,* which incorporates a multitude of personal qualities, and *player* in the narrower sense of striking the ball. Hogan, like Vardon before him, set an entirely new standard in perfection of striking a golf ball. After his tragic accident and torturous recovery, Hogan was persuaded that his crown would never be complete without the jewel of a British Open. So in 1953, having taken the Masters and U.S. Open, he arrived in Scotland, bent on the classic triple. Fittingly for a golfer of his caliber, the Open was at Carnoustie. No worthier test could be devised. The championship itself was not particularly exciting. Drama in golf is bred of mistakes and Hogan gave an almost flawless exhibition of ac-

curate stroke play. His putting, never much more than adequate and later to become a private cross, was unexceptional, but he still won by four shots and a record aggregate. He returned home to a ticker-tape welcome. If his name on the Open Championship trophy confirmed his reputation, it also enhanced the championship itself. For over a hundred years every golfer with any pretensions to greatness has won that old claret jug. Without the name of Ben Hogan engraved on it, the cup would surely be incomplete.

The young Australian Peter Thomson now stepped from the wings and took the center of the Open stage. Three victories in succession and then, at intervals, two more threatened Vardon's record of six

A water-logged Henry Cotton, winner of the Open at Carnoustie, 1937, after what he described as the round of his life. Above: Fifth Open championship for Peter Thomson, at Royal Birkdale in 1965.

championships and firmly established Thomson among the greats. If his reputation must be qualified, as a small-ball player preeminent on fast links courses, this was a matter of his own choosing. As a golfer Thomson's career has been hampered by a high intelligence and firmly held opinions; prejudices might not be too strong a word in some cases. In addition, he reproached himself for playing a frivolous game while the world fought and starved. And when he did rationalize his life and accepted that his contribution to society was a valuable one, he nevertheless refused to sublimate his personal prejudices in a singleminded assault on golfing fame and wealth. A manager would have been mad with frustration at Thomson's refusal to exploit his own talents. As noted earlier, he did not like the big ball or the modern style of watered courses. As a result his American appearances were strictly limited, and because he did not like American courses and the trend to target golf, the legend grew that he was anti-American. However, on the fast links of Britain he was supreme. The traditionalist in him responded to the challenge of running up approaches to the hard greens, and this type of golf particularly suited his game, which is based on touch, instinct, and improvisation.

The Thomson era coincided with a decline in the standing of the Open, not that this in any way detracts from his achievements. The championship organization was sketchy and old-fashioned and the prize money poor. The Open had failed to keep pace with the developments in golf and few American players felt it worthwhile to make the trip.

All that began to change with the rise of Arnold Palmer. His name was selling clubs in Britain and the manufacturer, Dunlop, wanted him to be seen by the home fans. Besides, like Hogan, Palmer was hungry to prove himself a true champion. His victory in 1961 at Royal Birkdale, and even more dramatically at Troon the following year, restored the prestige of the Open and probably contributed to a new dyna-

mism within the R. and A. No longer was it enough for the Open to be the oldest championship in golf. A gentlemanly revolution within the R. and A. brought a determination that the Open must become the best championship in every way. Many people within golf would claim that during the following ten years most of those worthy aims were achieved.

The roll of American Open champions is itself a potted history of the competition. The first National Open, celebrating the inauguration of the USGA in 1894, was a match-play event, and in the final Willie Dunn beat Willie Campbell and won $150. Those names, like their successors Rawlins, Foulis, Herd, Anderson, and Auchterlonie, have about them the salty tang of the Scottish fishing villages of their origins. Some of the same names occur in the early records of the British Open—Dunn, Campbell, Herd, Anderson, and Auchterlonie, all well-known Scottish golfing families. The U.S. Open was largely an annual gathering of the immigrant clansmen of the next generation.

One family, the Carnoustie Smiths, was represented by three brothers, Willie, Alex, and Macdonald. The last was generally judged to be the most accomplished, although he was the only one not to win a title. However, the outstanding player of this era was Willie Anderson, who took the Open four times. Like Young Tom Morris, he died at an early age (thirty-two), leaving to conjecture what further honors might have been his. The only golfers with any chance of breaking the Scottish-American monopoly were visiting pros from Britain, such as Harry Vardon, who managed the considerable feat of missing a two-inch putt on the last green of the Chicago Club, in Wheaton, Illinois, but won by two strokes.

The one pitfall in reading American social history into the names of Open winners is Johnny McDermott, who might be assumed to have been another immigrant. In fact, McDermott was American-born and obsessed with the ambition to prove that

203

Jack Nicklaus with an unplayable lie in the Piccadilly tournament at Wentworth, 1966. After dropping clear, Nicklaus claimed further relief from an obstructing advertisement but the referee refused.

home-bred golfers could play as well, and better, than the foreigners. In 1910 he finished in a tie with two of the Carnoustie Smiths, Alex and Macdonald, but could only beat one of them in the play-off. McDermott was involved in another play-off the following year (against Mike Brady and the Englishman George Sargent), and this time he came through to end the British supremacy. He won again in 1912, just to emphasize the close of the era. But was it really ended? The next year, 1913, the formidable pair of Harry Vardon and Ted Ray, the colossus of British golf and the reigning Open champion, were entered for the National Open at the Country Club in Brookline, Massachusetts. McDermott, the wiry bantamweight with the peppery temperament, was generally regarded as America's best bet to give the invaders a run for their money. But a flashy young braggart from Rochester, with slicked-down hair and an outrageously colorful outfit, showed up to register his entry and announce that he had come to help lick the British. Everyone laughed. Who was this brash kid, anyway? Hagen? Never heard of him. For that matter, nobody had heard of a certain twenty-year-old clerk who had been persuaded to file his entry by a USGA official. The organizers were so anxious to make a show of the Open that they were even encouraging unknown amateurs to have a go. When the name of Francis Ouimet began to appear among the leaders, few people knew how to pronounce it (Wee-met). As expected, Vardon and Ray dominated the qualifying rounds, but both Ouimet and Hagen managed to survive.

In the championship proper, McDermott's game was off and at the halfway stage Vardon led by two shots over Ray. It was, it seemed, the old story. Who was left to mount a challenge? No one of consequence. The local amateur with the funny name was still in sight and so—barely—was that kid Hagen. But golf galleries knew that hot rounds by unknowns meant very little. When it came to the pressures of the closing stages it was the hard men who held on. So even when

Ryder Cup at Royal Birkdale, 1965, with Arnold Palmer (l.) and Don January. Invincible on this occasion, the Americans returned to the same course four years later. That match resulted in a historic tie.

*What the Ryder Cup means to Britain: Thousands turned
out in 1965 to watch Dave Marr (above on left) and
Arnold Palmer, and (r.) a slightly pensive foursome
in Tony Lema, Gene Littler, Don January, and Billy Casper.*

Ouimet caught Vardon at the end of the third round, it was a cause for congratulations but hardly for hope.

In the last round Vardon, whose putting was always vulnerable, could make nothing of the sodden greens and was around in 79 for a total of 304. Ray tied, and the best possibility for a challenge seemed to lie with Hagen, who picked up four shots on par in three holes, and could conceivably join the leaders if he played out steadily. Hagen attempted a grandstand finish with a spectacular fairway wood, topped the ball feebly, and bowed out of the championship, to return presumably to the oblivion whence he had come. Predictably, the inexperienced Ouimet was making a hash of his last round in accordance with the honored conventions of precocious youth. He was out in 43 and

needed to improve on that performance by eight strokes coming home to catch Vardon and Ray. On that rain-soaked course and by the way he was playing, his chances seemed slim, indeed. Ouimet himself was not daunted. This shy, quiet young man had a plan. He calculated that if he could birdie the two short holes and get par figures on the others he could do it. Like all such plans on the golf course, it went wrong. He got his first 2 by chipping into the hole, but at the next short hole he had to sink a 9-footer to save par. The second birdie would have to be found elsewhere. It came on the 17th, after a string of pars helped erode the Britishers' lead. He made a 20-foot downhill putt, which was blessed with a certain degree of luck, and assured himself a tie with a 5-footer on the last. He had

done it, although a good many spectators did not see his triumph because they had gone home, believing his cause to be hopeless. The uproar among the three thousand who remained was unprecedented in the decorous history of the Country Club and this euphoric moment was not time for realistic thoughts about the play-off. Ouimet still had to meet Vardon and Ray.

It was expected that the youngster would suffer a reaction and collapse in the decisive encounter. In the morning Ouimet hit a few practice shots on the 18th fairway (which would disqualify him under to-day's rules), and then joined his opponents on the first tee. So far events had gone like the plot for a story in a boys' magazine, and a magazine sponsored by the League of Purity at that. Ouimet, the humble lad whose

lips had never been sullied by tobacco, alcohol, or pro-fanity, had matched the foreign invaders at their own game. Purity and innocence must surely triumph in this coming denouement. Now, however, the story line deflected into farce. Ouimet's ten-year-old caddie, Eddie Lowery, handed him the driver with the stirring advice, "Be sure and keep your eye on the ball, Francis."

All his life Ouimet remained modest and unassuming and never lost the air of a quiet country boy. But like many another quiet country boy, he was nobody's mug even at the age of twenty. He was a fine player and exceptionally composed on the course no matter how bleak the situation. In terms of pressure, Vardon and Ray, with everything to lose and nothing to gain, were at a disadvantage. Ray put himself out of

209

In love with success: Gary Player admires
the PGA trophy at Newton Square, Pennsylvania, 1962, and
Tony Jacklin is escorted by the Lancashire
police after his Open victory at Lytham in 1969.

the reckoning as the play-off reached the critical stage. Vardon drove into a bunker at the 17th as Ouimet stroked in an 18-footer for a birdie. If anyone broke, it was Vardon, with a 6 at the last, while Ouimet made the coolest of 4s to complete the most famous victory in golf's long history.

Some American golf historians, such as the admirable Charles Price, are undecided about the impact on American golf of Ouimet's triumph, pointing out that it was to be many years before the ascendancy of American golf was reflected in results. Obviously, it did not make the American pros better players over-

night. The immediate and overwhelming effect was psychological. Proof had been given in the most dramatic possible manner that the native game could go it alone. McDermott and Ouimet had provided a glimpse of a new Jerusalem, an all-American capital of the golfing world. And that is exactly what happened. In suceeding years the Anglo-Scottish domination of the National Open gave way to foreign-sounding names like Dutra, Manero, Guldahl, Boros, and Venturi. These were the second and third generations of Americans to whom Italy, Poland, and Hungary were just places on the map. Oddly enough, the more the list of competi-

tors for the Open read like a roll call at the United Nations, the more American it became. It is still very much a domestic championship. While there may be thirty different nationalities represented in a British Open championship, it would be unusual to have ten nationalities in a U.S. Open field. As long as this remains the case, and there is no good reason why it should, the National Open cannot be regarded as an unofficial world championship. In many other respects, however, its preeminence is secure. In the matter of organization and the preparation of courses, the USGA sets the standards which the rest of the world tries—

and in most cases fails by a wide margin—to follow.

The Masters is undoubtedly one of the modern classics, accepted as an essential trick for the Grand Slam, and yet it has no official status. Technically it is a club invitational tournament. The factor which gives the Masters its unique status can be expressed in one word: continuity. All the elements of the tournament's success owe something to the fact that it is held at the same time of year on the same course with the same officials. It would be absurd to suggest that mistakes and snags do not occur at Augusta, but continuity of organization means that the

Engrossed crowds watch the agonies of the short 16th during the 1971 Masters at Augusta. If and when the players safely carry the water, they face ordeal of trying to hole out on the fast, two-tier green.

Color in the galleries—including modesty
carried to Victorian lengths with a knitted cover for
periscope. This, then, is California, land of the
beautiful people, and the 1972 U.S. Open at Pebble Beach.

same mistake is not allowed to happen twice.

An efficient organization is not of itself enough to make a great tournament. For that you need a strong field and a course good enough to ensure a worthy winner every time. As for the course, the seeds were planted a hundred years before Bobby Jones and his friends bought the site in 1930, because this was an old tree and shrub nursery. So the Augusta National was blessed with instant maturity in the stands of great Georgia pine and the wealth of decorative shrubs. Over the years the club has built permanent crowd facilities, such as grandstands and refreshment huts with their inevitable corollaries, and camouflaged them to blend as unobtrusively as possible into the landscape. Continuity provides that bonus. Augusta does not need flapping canvas to mount the Masters and so avoids the circus feeling of most golf promotions. The atmosphere of the Masters is more that of a garden party.

We have discussed the quality of the course in an earlier chapter. Small changes are made from time to time to keep it up to the highest championship standard as golf equipment and techniques improve. For example, when Jack Nicklaus began to flout the authority of a fairway bunker by carrying it with the contemptuous power of his drive, the bunker was moved 20 yards farther from the tee. As for the quality of the field, Bobby Jones' reputation gave the first invitations the power of a royal command, and in due course there evolved a codified system by which golfers qualified for an invitation.

With organization, the course, and the field, the Masters needed one more ingredient to achieve international stature. It was only a matter of time before the missing ingredient—a tradition of greatness—began to accrue to the new tournament. In its second year, the Masters produced the most famous single shot in the history of American golf. Craig Wood was in with a total of 282 and looking safe enough when Gene Sarazen addressed his four-wood to the ball for a 220-yard approach to the par-5 15th. He needed to clip three shots off par on those testing last four holes to tie Wood's score and he appeared a good bet to pick up one of them as his approach shot bored straight at the flag. The ball carried the water, pitched, rolled, and dropped into the hole for a double eagle, or albatross in the British idiom. With that one masterly shot, Sarazen had made up his three shots and he matched par over the remaining holes for a tie. He won the play-off easily and the legend of the Masters was born.

Wood's turn came six years later, but meanwhile, in 1937, Byron Nelson had his dramatic day. He seemed to be coasting home in the wake of the front-running Ralph Guldahl. At the short 12th Guldahl had a 5 and he dropped another shot to par at the next hole. Nelson had a birdie and an eagle on these same two holes, picking up six strokes in the process, and won by two shots.

Nelson made more Masters history in 1942, when he had to play off after a tie with the redoubtable Ben Hogan. It began to look ominous when Hogan went three shots ahead over the opening five holes. Over the next eleven holes Hogan was rock steady and one under par, but Nelson, in an inspired burst, caught him nonetheless and had a two-shot lead as they teed up for the 17th. Hogan got back one stroke but Nelson hung on for a single-shot triumph.

Hogan again got the worst of a play-off, against Sam Snead in 1954, the year after his second victory. In all, Hogan was runner-up four times, a remarkable record of consistency, second only to that of four-time winner Arnold Palmer.

Jack Nicklaus won his first Masters in 1963 at the age of twenty-three. The wind was high and so were the scores, but two years later conditions were perfect and Nicklaus produced one of the great tournament performances of modern golf. His score

*Like a matador poised for the kill—Lee
Trevino plumb-lines his putter during 1971 Westchester
Classic while the aficionados await moment of
truth. This time truth turned sour—he missed the cut.*

of 271 was unprecedented—it is usually ten shots higher. (His own winning aggregates on other occasions were 288 and 286.)

Although the story of a great tournament must necessarily be mainly about winners, there is a place for losers and surely none is more poignant than Roberto de Vicenzo in 1968. The popular Argentinian is one of the purest strikers of a ball that golf has seen. Only Snead has won more tournaments, a statistic which must be subject to ratification, since de Vicenzo himself is not sure of his record after twenty years of globe-trotting. He is content to let other people concern themselves with details of that sort. And it was just such a happy-go-lucky attitude which was his undoing at Augusta. In the last round an audience of thousands (plus millions of TV watchers) saw him tie with Bob Goalby. But his playing partner inadvertently marked him down for a 4 on a hole where he had taken 3. De Vicenzo signed his card after a perfunctory glance at the total (which was correct). However, golfers are not responsible for returning a correct total; their duty is to sign for the scores at the eighteen individual holes, and under the rules of golf de Vicenzo had attested to that spurious 4 and it had to stand. So Goalby was the winner and a most unlucky one at that. Through no fault of his own he was widely regarded as having won by default, the champion by a technicality. De Vicenzo was overwhelmed by public sympathy and stole every headline. Winning the Masters is usually a springboard for a fortune in endorsements, exhibitions, and advertising. Goalby, although he had undoubtedly won, was not seen as the winner. He wanted a special dispensation to allow de Vicenzo's score to be adjusted, so that they could play off and give him the chance to prove himself the unchallenged Masters winner. Unfortunately, the rules forbid such incidents to be resolved in accordance with the dictates of common sense and natural justice. A marker's error and an idiotically inflexible law made this a hol-

low victory for Goalby. But the next year, as was to be expected on past Masters form, a small enclosure was erected behind the 18th green where an official carefully checked every card with competitors before they were permitted to add their signatures. In accordance with the Masters tradition the same mistake was not to be allowed to happen twice.

The Professional Golfers' Association Championship is the fourth of the classics and it must be said that for some years it held this elevated status under false pretenses. The original championship, instituted in 1916, was a match-play event. In man-to-man golf the quality of the course is of secondary importance, since it is the same for both players and, given the usual element of chance in an eighteen-hole match, the better player will win. The interplay of personality becomes a factor, as does the opponent's performance.

In stroke-play events the purpose is to set an examination, and in order to produce a worthy winner there must be a worthy course. It should test the player's skills with every club and every variety of shot. In stroke play a golfer must ignore what his playing partner is doing (unless they are both challenging over the closing holes), while in match play a man's tactics will be dictated by his opponent's fortunes. The better player will (or should) win whether they are playing a good course or a bad one.

An obvious example of how tactics are dictated by the progress of a match would be when an opponent hits a superb, or lucky, approach shot right by the flag, especially to a tightly guarded green. Instead of aiming for the center of the green, which would be the usual practice in a stroke-play competition, the player must now suppress his golfing instincts, ignore the dangers, and go for the flag himself.

Again, if a man finds himself four down with six holes to play there is no point in playing conservative golf. He has to gamble. At a tight hole, where he would normally use an iron off the tee (and

Master of the expansive gesture, Trevino hurls his cap into the Royal Birkdale gallery after sinking the putt that won him the 1971 Open championship, by a shot from the Formosan Lu Liang Huan.

which is exactly what his opponent will be doing), he must decide whether to risk the driver and win a possible advantage. Nearly every professional announces before a match that he intends to "play the course" and forget about what his opponent is doing. Yet nearly always those brave words have to be eaten before the match is over. The circumstances of the match force him to revise his game plan.

The roll of winners in the match-play era shows that the best man did indeed win. Walter Hagen, whose bursting confidence gave him the equivalent of a two-up start against most opponents, won four times in a row; Gene Sarazen took three titles; and the names of Sam Snead, Ben Hogan, and Byron Nelson all appear more than once on the winners' roll.

In 1958, under pressure from television, which cannot cope with match-play golf, the championship format changed to four rounds of stroke play. It thus became indistinguishable from any of the other tour events, especially as it was frequently played on courses which could not be considered of championship standard, either in their intrinsic layout or their preparation.

For a time the importance of the PGA championship lay mainly in the fact that the winner was exempted for life from prequalifying for all PGA-sponsored events. It was thus a valuable title to win, but as a golfing accomplishment it really meant very little more than any other bread-and-butter tournament. The old tradition withered and the only new tradition which developed was the unwelcome superstition that the victor would not win another tournament. This notion arose from the experience of players such as Bobby Nichols, Dave Marr, Al Geiberger, and Don January, who all had prolonged spells in the doldrums after becoming PGA champion. Then, after the revolution within the PGA, which resulted in the formation of an autonomous Tournament Players' Division, the fortunes of the championship began to

219

Rivals as a partnership—Lee Trevino and Jack Nicklaus confer on the line of a putt during the World Cup at Palm Beach, 1971. So what went wrong (above)? Nothing serious. Despite this setback the Americans won the cup.

revive. The improvement stemmed from the appointment of Joe Dey, a former director of USGA, as commissioner. All Dey's instincts and experience insisted that a championship must be played on tough courses, prepared so that only outstanding players could come through. It would obviously take a few years for his policy to burnish the championship's reputation.

Fifty years ago the Amateur Championships of Britain and the United States ranked as classics, and were indeed elements in Bobby Jones' Grand Slam. In those days there was little incentive for a gifted young amateur to turn professional. John Ball, the great Hoylake golfer, competed in the Amateur for fifty years, winning it eight times, and since he also won an Open, he was in his prime clearly a match for any pro. The standard in the first Amateur Championships was probably higher than in the first Opens. Although this trend was reversed, and decisively so, as the years went by, we have the evidence of Bobby Jones that as late as 1930 it was just as difficult to win an Amateur as an Open. As pro golf became more lucrative, however, the Amateur championships declined in importance, since the best young players were being skimmed off every year. In America the Amateur Championship was changed to stroke play in 1965, in step with the fashion, and to a large extent it became an initiation test for embryo professionals. In 1973 the U.S. Amateur reverted to a match-play championship.

The true amateur (in the sense of a weekend golfer who plays for fun) can hardly hope to compete against the young tigers from college golf teams who are almost full-time players and come to the championship hardened to the rigors of tournament play. The same kind of thing, in a modified degree, is happening to the British Amateur, although it is not so apparent, since Britain offers no golf scholarships. As in most things, British golf takes its lead from the States—the good ideas normally take ten years to cross the Atlantic, the bad ideas ten seconds—and it is

Palmer's unique style: The high flourish (actually the result of a correction during the swing required by an unorthodox take-away), and naked emotions are his trademarks. Here, the Westchester Classic, 1971.

221

only a matter of time until the British Amateur becomes the steepest nursery slope before graduation to professionalism.

With the huge expansion of golf in the postwar years, a subtle evolutionary process began to divide it into virtually two different games. On the one hand, we have golf as a recreational activity, grown to an enormous degree but still basically the same as always. On the other hand, there is professional golf, which year by year becomes further removed from the amateur or country-club variety. Once the two worlds of golf were inextricably linked; the pros were a part of the clubs and deeply involved with them, and the game they played was not so different from that of the more skilled members.

Today, with a handful of exceptions, amateur golf cannot begin to compete with tournament professionalism. The gulf in playing standards is vast and growing. Superficially, it is not easy to detect the extent of the difference. After all, there are plenty of amateurs who regularly return scores at their home clubs which compare favorably enough with the scores on the pro tour. But a 72 in the club championship cannot be compared with a 72 in, say, the Westchester Classic, because the circumstances are so widely different. And to understand that difference we must examine something of the structure of the pro tour. How, for instance, does a likely young amateur become a tournament professional?

The days are long gone when all he needed was a bag of clubs, a good swing, and unlimited ambition. Modern golf is an expensive business. It costs about $500 a week on tour, and to play forty tournaments requires an outlay of $20,000. So you finance the second tournament from your first week's winnings? Oh, no, the PGA won't allow that. You have to prove that you can afford to play the circuit before you are allowed onto it. But, says the rookie, if I had $20,000 I would not *need* to turn pro. I haven't got it. Then, says

The victory salute as Palmer wins the 1971
Westchester. This picture really needs scoring for massed
chorus of delirious fans roaring appreciation. For
personal popularity Palmer is winner every time he plays.

the PGA, find it. In the majority of cases, the youngster has to start off with a backer and it is here that his troubles are likely to begin. There are philanthropists who are prepared to give a young golfer a start in life without seeking any return on their money. However, in life there are few genuine fairy godmothers. Sponsors are mostly businessmen who are looking for a profit. And they know rather more about the intricacies of drawing up contracts than golfers do.

As a result, many players discover that they have signed away their lives. At least one recruit to the circuit finished with nothing, although he won $65,000 in his first season, simply because he had not read the small print in his sponsor contract. Another player won $100,000 three years in a row—most of it unfortunately for the sponsor who had him tied up in a legal stranglehold.

Let us assume that the young player has solved the cash situation, possibly by putting himself in the hands of a reputable manager. Now he has to submit his golf to close official scrutiny. It is now that he comes up against that agonizing prefix "pre"—in the first instance, a prequalifying school. This is a regional preliminary tournament to determine which players are suitable candidates for the PGA's qualifying school. It is the first mesh of the grading system which ensures that only golfers of outstanding skills join the tour. If our lad safely passes this test he may enter the qualifying school at PGA headquarters.

The term "PGA school" is somewhat misleading since the element of instruction is small. And while the candidates are given a certain amount of lecture-room advice on professionalism—how to deport themselves on the course, how to talk to the press, how much to pay caddies—the one thing they are not taught is how to play golf. They know that already. Teaching golf is part of the PGA's function, but this is conducted through its club-professional members. Pros receive advice on how to teach others and what to teach others,

but by the time the embryo tournament player is ready to go to the PGA school he must be a player of very considerable skill. The PGA will not undertake to teach him to achieve pro caliber. For many school candidates, how to play and how to compete are lessons learned during their years on college golf teams. University golfers get the benefit of four years or so of intensive coaching, as well as considerable experience of competitive pressure in college team matches, major amateur tournaments, and possibly as members of international teams.

The main function of the school is to provide an examination of playing ability in the form of a six-round, stroke-play tournament. The results are decided by the number of places available on tour. If six players have dropped out of the circuit, the leading six candidates will be chosen as replacements. The successful ones are given probationary cards as members of the Tournament Players' Division, and these TPD cards are their passports to fame and fortune. Like passports, they simply allow the bearers to proceed to the next stage. In their case it is a PGA tournament or, more precisely, the prequalifying round of a tournament, usually known as Heartbreak Monday.

There may be two hundred golfers taking part, and because of exemptions and invitations, there may be only six vacancies in the field for a particular tournament. It has often been remarked that a golfer has to play better to get into a tournament than to win it. That may be true. Certainly the pressures are much more intense.

Let us assume that our boy manages to get one of those six places. He is now "in," one of perhaps one hundred and forty-four golfers with a chance to win some real money. It is still only a chance. First, he has to play well enough in the first two rounds to survive the cut. Now, and only now, can he hope to cover his expenses or, just possibly, make a profit on the week's $500 outlay. Failure at any point means going back to the previous stage. Miss that cut and you are back to prequalifying the following Monday. And possibly the next. And if you do not show progress the PGA may withdraw your precious TPD card in the annual review. No wonder most recruits drop out.

Some make it to the level where they can live on their winnings—but no higher. A tiny proportion—and it is much smaller than the opulence the official money lists suggest—becomes wealthy from playing golf.

To the sporting public pro golf is about winning tournaments. To the pros themselves, however, the purpose is to win money. That means it is far better to finish in the first twenty or so week after week than to bring off one flashy victory and do nothing for the rest of the season. For many pros winning is not the name of the game at all. They do not want to win. The winner must endure special pressures, and make speeches and submit to being lionized. That is all very well for those who like it, but many pros are not temperamentally suited to the limelight. They prefer the comparative calm of the second echelon and the motto: Play steady, eat regular. Year after year they pick up official winnings of $50,000–$70,000, which is not spectacular once they have deducted their expenses, since it costs everyone the same amount, according to life style, to play the tour. But it should be remembered that official winnings are by no means the same as total income. Every tour player has contracts with equipment and clothing manufacturers. They all pick up useful supplements from pro-ams and exhibition matches. There is no formula for computing how much a pro can earn in "unofficial" money, but a conservative estimate in most cases would be to double the figure for official winnings.

Among the stars the official money is the least part of their income. More than one golfer has signed his name to a million-dollar contract. For such men the act of airily donating a winning check to charity is an expansive gesture but under modern tax structures not a particularly generous one.

On the surface the pro tour is friendly, easygoing, and relaxed. Basically it is as tough a rat race as modern life has to offer. The amateur who picks up his newspaper and remarks that he could shoot better golf than those guys on tour should pause and consider the prospects very carefully indeed before he attempts to put that boast to the test. It is not just a different game. It is not a game at all.

That being the case, it is hardly appropriate for us club golfers to try to model ourselves on the professionals. Perhaps it is inevitable that we should watch Jack Nicklaus and then attempt to copy him; all the same, it is ridiculous. While there may be very good reasons for Nicklaus to pace out his shots to the green, or to spend two minutes sizing up a putt, it does not follow that we lesser players will obtain the slightest benefit from such practices. We will continue to do so, of course, and by aping professional golf we will continue to obscure the gulf which divides us from the pros. Logically we ought to accept the fact that we are participating in an utterly different activity.

If we could swallow our pride and absorb that distinction, we might begin to search for solutions for our problems. Try as he might, the 22-handicapper will not get down to 20 by copying Arnold Palmer's swing. He has a good chance of making a dramatic improvement if he deliberately swings three times as slowly as Palmer. And if at the same time he goes through the card before his round and writes "par-5" against every hole longer than 400 yards—and adjusts his game accordingly—his scores will immediately improve. Alas, human nature does not work like that. Self-deception is altogether too powerful for us to concede that those guys are playing a different game. We will struggle on, grotesque parodies of our heroes. It will cost us dearly in side bets and drinks—but that serves us right for being such blinkered dupes.

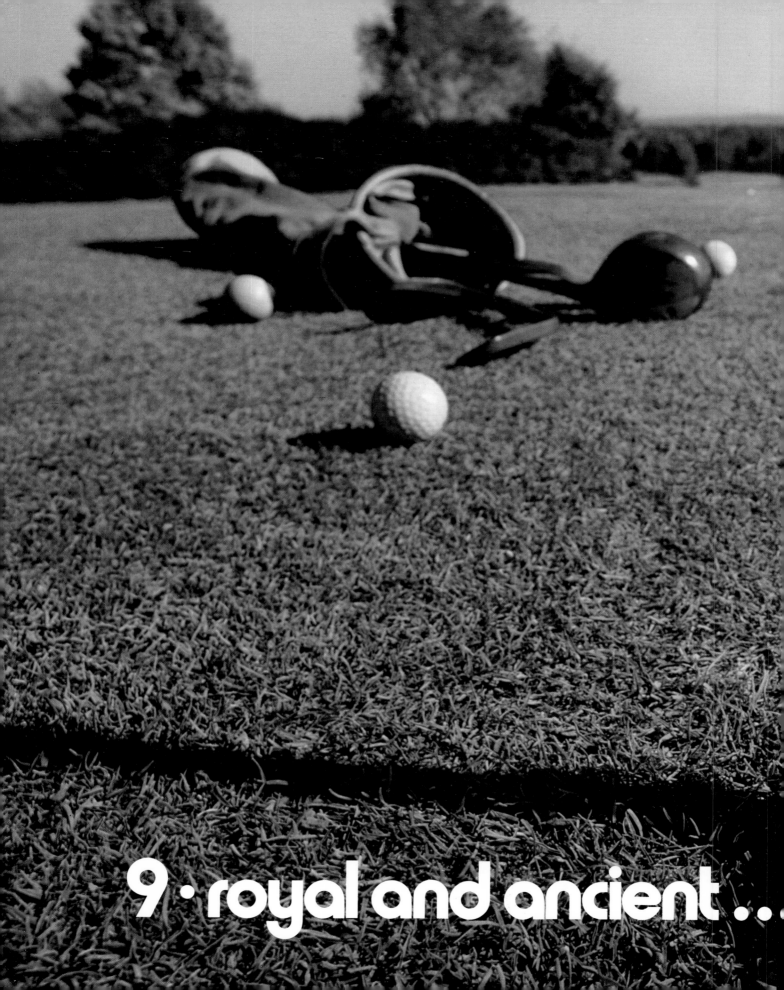

9 · royal and ancient . . .

and antic

When it came to filling out his entry form for the British Open of 1965, Walter Danecki had a brief crisis of conscience. He had to state whether he was an amateur or a professional, and that was a difficult decision for forty-three-year-old Walter, a mail sorter from Milwaukee who played weekend golf on a municipal course and who proposed to take a holiday in Britain. He also proposed to play in the Open. This was straightforward enough: Walter's amateur status was unstained. As he later explained, he did not charge if he gave a lesson. On the other hand, Walter believed he could beat Arnold Palmer and, what's more, he was determined to win the Open. "I wanted the crock of gold, so my conscience made me write down 'professional,'" he said.

Walter had made inquiries about joining the PGA and had been put off the idea because of the stipulation of a five-year apprenticeship. "What I'll do is win one of the big ones," he told himself, "and then they'll have to let me in." Boy, would his friends be impressed when he came home with the trophy. And if perchance some unforeseen catastrophe beyond his control should rob him of his triumph, putting him in second place, say, or even third, then the whole venture would be his little secret. Nobody at home need ever know. So, true to the spirit of the rules of amateurism governing "professional intent," Walter filed his entry as a pro, and the R. and A., which at that time did not scrutinize credentials very closely, accepted it.

Walter was drawn to play the prequalifying rounds at Hillside, just over the fence from the Birkdale championship course. Hillside is generally reckoned to be a few shots easier than Birkdale. Against the par of 70, Walter and his playing partner reckoned that two 75s would be good enough to qualify. Walter went round in 108. Officials of the R. and A. thought that Walter would quietly fold his tent and creep away after this debacle. They arranged for a substitute to play the second round with his partner.

Next morning Walter presented himself on the tee, not a whit abashed. "I don't like to quit. I like to golf and that's what I came to do," he said. This time he had a considerable gallery in attendance. He started with two 7s and an 8 and then settled down with two solid bogey 5s. Then a 7 and a 9 were followed by two more 5s to put him out in 58. Perhaps that total unnerved him, because he started back 9, 6, 10 before he got it going again for an inward half of 55. Round in 113, or 43 over par, to make a two-round aggregate of 221. He missed qualifying by just 70 strokes. But the indomitable Walter wasn't making any excuses. Far from it. "I want to say that your small ball is right for this sort of course," he said. "If I had been playing our bigger ball I would have been all over the place."

God bless you, Walter. The world would be a poorer place without people like you. Happily, golf is full of Walters. No game is as rich in human eccentricity as golf, and its foibles are carefully recorded in *The Golfer's Handbook*. This work, which is published in Glasgow every year, is basically devoted to golfing records and useful information, but the best of it is a section headed "Interesting Facts, Feats and Extraordinary Occurrences in the Game." There follows a great number of subdivisions under such headings as "Spectators interfering with balls," and "Balls in strange places." The entries, which cover more than a hundred pages of fine print, are presented in deadpan, almost telegraphic fashion, although occasionally the editors reveal a flash of personal opinion. For instance, under "Freak Matches," there is an item reading, "In United States competitions with nondescript hazards, such as suspended barrels to be played through and gates played around, are frequently held"—and here one can detect a pursing of the puritanical lips—"to provide what are supposed to be amusing variations of the game."

For the most part this section is a casebook of golf lunacy. Here an eminent violinist plays a

Simplicity of golf when the century was young—just an easily carried bag of a few clubs, bramble-pattern rubber-core ball, and the prospect of forty-five holes of golf in a day.

228

match attired in a suit of armour. "He was beaten by 2 and 1" the item adds, which we cannot help feeling served him right. A millionaire travels between shots by helicopter and another rare spirit plays a round by divebombing a course in a light airplane and hurling golf balls at the greens. He completed eighteen holes in 29 shots. Golfers challenge archers, javelin throwers, racquets players, and flyfishermen and hardly a day passes, it seems, without somebody attempting a speed round or a cross-country marathon.

The editors reserve their greatest enthusiasm for disasters. The lady who required 166 strokes at a short hole gets a fat entry, and fatal accidents on the course are recorded in morbid detail. The carnage caused to fish, birds, and animals by golf balls gets a separate section. But aficionados of these golfing curios were dismayed by recent editorial pruning of the section "Hit by ball—distance of rebound." In earlier editions this was a rich treasury of tasteless trivia. The record was held by an unnamed South African caddie who, on September 28, 1913, was struck just above the right temple by a ball driven by Edward Sladwick. The rebound was measured at 75 yards. This shattered the record. See here, the longest rebound in the book is Barton, playing at Machrie, beaned a caddie named John McNiven. Out came the tape measure to record a rebound of 42 yards, 2 feet, 10 inches. We can imagine the excitement as Mr. Barton and his friends consulted *The Golfer's Handbook.* "We did it! It's a new world record. See here, the longest rebound in the book is thirty-four yards, set up way back in August, 1908, at Blairgowrie at the ninth hole." How transient are such moments of triumph. Just twenty-seven days later the title went to Mr. Sladwick. Still, Barton retains the British native record.

It is now useless to consult the *Handbook* if you should have the good fortune to catch a caddie flush on the forehead. The records have been withdrawn. You will be all right if you step into a bunker and sink waist deep. You will find such deeds in an appropriate section, but you are doomed to disappointment. On July 11, 1931, at Rose Bay, New South Wales, Mr. D. J. Bayley MacArthur did the same thing, only he sank to the armpits. If your ball impales itself on a hatpin without dislodging the hat, or pierces a spectator's topper, or lodges in a donkey's ear, or drops down a chimney into a pot of Irish stew bubbling on the hearth, you may make it among similar examples. But rebounds are out.

As for freakish scoring, you will have to do something really spectacular to qualify. It's no good starting off 1, 2, 3, 4, 5, 6, for instance, because it has been done already. If your opponent holes out with his tee shot you should not delude yourself with the heady thought that it would be quite unprecedented to do an ace yourself and halve the hole. It has happened before. Several times. Almost commonplace. What about a hole in one at successive holes? Sorry, it's been done: in 1971 during a PGA tournament in the British circuit. John Hudson, making a rare tournament appearance as a break from his duties as a club pro, holed out at a short hole at Norwich golf club. The next hole, played from an elevated tee and partly blind from a stand of trees, measures 311 yards. Hudson cracked one with his driver, although most of the field was playing discreetly short because of the tightness of the approach to the greens, and holed out.

For sheer luck it would be hard to surpass the experience of the golfer who sliced his drive at Prestwick's first hole. The ball flew out-of-bounds, hit the railway line, and rebounded into play. He sliced his approach shot. Again it carried the O.B. fence, again it hit the railway line, and this time it rebounded onto the green and rolled into the hole. Fair enough, but a similar incident had an unhappy sequel at Los Angeles in 1950. Bob Geared sliced his tee shot at the 425-yard second hole and his ball bounced on the road and landed in a passing truck. The driver tossed the ball back by the green and it went into the hole. The committee heartlessly ruled that he should have played another ball off the tee under the O.B. rule.

Not every curious incident finds its way into the *Handbook*. Possibly because they do not have a subsection for "Sexual Deviants on the Links" the editors missed, for instance, the Effingham affair. A foursome of lady members was playing on the exclusive suburban course at Effingham, near London. They were putting out when a man wearing a bowler hat and nothing else sprang from the bushes. Undaunted, the lady captain demanded sternly, "Are you a member?" and receiving no satisfactory reply—it would hardly have done to offend, say, an influential committee chairman—dispatched the intruder with a sharp blow from her eight-iron. All golfers will understand why she did not risk damaging her putter on such an unyielding target.

In the normal course of events sex has very little association with golf. That statement may provoke boisterous laughter in ten thousand clubhouses, and I quite understand. Every club has its scandals from time to time, but this is essentially *après*-golf and has no direct connection with the game. On the course men and women tend to avoid each other's company, no matter what they may do later. The golf is the thing at the time. Among the professionals a few, such as Walter Hagen, could cast an appraising eye over the galleries and chat up a dolly while playing an important match. But, generally, the pros keep their minds on the game. What they do later is their business and no lurid revelations will be made here.

In one part of the world sex and golf do coexist. The wealthy mandarin golfers of Taiwan have evolved a local custom which may surprise visitors. When two western businessmen were invited to join two merchants for a round, they were only too glad and readily agreed to play for "the usual stakes," thinking this would mean a $5 nassau or something of that

order. They won, rather easily, and accepted an invitation to play again the next day on the same terms. They won again and the Chinese said they would send the winnings round to their hotel. That evening the businessmen were duly paged and found in the hotel lobby fourteen giggling girls who announced that they had come to give the golfers their bath. Somehow it is difficult to imagine the practice spreading.

Women generally have been the second-class citizens of golf. Although there is abundant evidence of their interest in the game, they were less than welcome in many clubs for many years. Only in the United States, even today, have women golfers won equality. There are a few men-only clubs in America and some lesser examples of discrimination can be discovered, but generally speaking American women golfers have achieved a freedom that is the envy of their overseas sisters. If they occasionally feel slighted, they might reflect on the situation elsewhere. In Australia, for example, the woman golfer is even denied her womanhood. Oh, she can join a golf club right enough if she is prepared to accept the condescending label of "associate." That is the word which marks her cramped and relatively inferior quarters in the clubhouse. And that is how she is called by the men—"I got held up at the ninth by a couple of associates"—as if she were a different species of lesser being. At that, she may be in a happier situation than her English counterpart who is dignified by the title "lady"—and by not much more in some clubs. Emancipation is spreading slowly in Britain but the process is fiercely resisted in certain bastions of male reaction where women are suffered, and themselves suffer.

In extreme instances, women are permitted to play the course, provided they stand meekly to the side of the fairway (preferably getting right out of sight) and allow any male match to go through with unimpeded progress, and provided they change their shoes in the car park and on no account attempt to set

Compare cartoonist Frank Reynolds' study of
"An Actor" in his 1933 series "Finishes of the Famous"
with the photograph of Arnold Palmer on
page 220—a case of life imitating art?

The Finishes of the Famous

A Politician   A Novelist   An Actor

A Scientist   A Welfare Worker   A Painter

A General   A Footballer   A Film-Star

foot in the clubhouse. The more usual restrictions consist of a kind of golfing purdah with the women confined to their own cramped quarters, forbidden to play at certain times, and subject to rigid rules of how they may dress. Some clubs maintain ludicrous regulations such as forbidding women to use a certain flight of steps in front of the club. Restrictions on the times when women may play are still fairly general. Most men see women's golf as a slightly frivolous, and miniaturized, version of their own game. And every golf club which permits women members can provide examples to support that smug theory. At the same time the theory is false. As in life, so in golf: Women are different. Mostly they play for different reasons. Psychiatrists are not notably reticent when it comes to talking rubbish, but none has yet suggested that women's golf involves an urge to display their virility. Women have no need to flex their muscles in public, and so from the very outset their basic reasons for playing golf are different. The appeal of the game lies in what it provides them—release from the domestic scene, companionship, fulfillment of the competitive instinct, and a congenial way of filling the waiting hours while husbands are at work. If that sounds patronizing, it is not meant to be. Once women become addicted to golf and set their minds seriously to it, they become highly proficient at the game.

Making due allowances for the disparity in horsepower, it is probably fair to say that the best women golfers achieve a higher level of skill at golf than the best men. At the professional level, and here we are talking mainly but not exclusively about the American women's golf circuit, the players at the strongest end of the scale are just about the equal of the shortest hitters on the men's tour.

But once the drives have been struck, the effective difference becomes progressively less marked through the range of clubs. A good woman player can use her four-wood to match the shot of a man playing the same distance with his four-iron. And once we get into the area of "touch shots" around the green, the women stars are not just the equals of the men but possibly their superiors. Where women golfers are at a disadvantage is in the controlled application of explosive power—as in bunkers and heavy rough—but they normally avoid such situations better than men because of greater accuracy.

Such a judgment must be generalized. It cannot be stressed too strongly that the distance a golf ball may be hit is governed less by sheer strength than by the speed of the clubhead. And clubhead speed can be generated by timing and technique in the hands of a physically frail woman, provided—and it is a proviso which is almost universally misunderstood, or ignored —that the weight of the club is reduced. It can be safely asserted with a mass of scientific proof that women's golf is grotesquely handicapped by the use of clubs which are totally unsuitable in weight. For confirmation we have only to watch women at golf. Control of the club is clearly essential. Yet when you see women playing golf it is obvious that very early in the stroke the club is swinging the women rather than the other way round. Clubmakers do employ women advisers, but they are famous players and as such exceptional. If women's golf is to be liberated, the battle must be waged on a much broader front than the area of male prejudice among club committees. They must get into the factories and insist on rational research and development. Burn your bras if you must, dear woman golfer (although *that* is probably the last garment for a golfer to discard), but for true liberation cast off the shackle of those 13-ounce drivers.

The search for improved performance on the golf course—and it should be made clear that we now are off the subject of sex—has strained the ingenuity of man to the limits of absurdity. Both the R. and A. and the USGA maintain black museums of illegal clubs which have been submitted by hopeful inventors.

Nearly all are designed on fallacious scientific theory. Most of them are weirdly contorted—the clubs, that is—and grossly violate the rule that clubs must conform to conventional shapes. It was in that spirit that the R. and A. banned the center-shafted Schenectady putter after the Australian-born American, Walter Travis, won the 1904 Amateur Championship at Sandwich with a putting display that was positively inhuman in its accuracy. Possibly there was an element of pique behind the decision since Travis, a man of waspish disposition, took no pains to conceal his animosity after being shabbily treated by the pompous officials. It was nearly fifty years before the center-shafted putter received official blessing.

The USGA was on rather firmer ground with its first decision concerning the form and make of golf clubs. In the inaugural U.S. Amateur Championship, won by the mighty Charles Macdonald, one of the competitors had a novel idea. Richard Peters insisted on putting with a billiard cue and was duly disqualified.

Many golfers have had the same idea since then and have tried to devise a putting method which uses the billiard-cue principle. It is, after all, the easiest way, some might even say the only way, of directing a ball at a target with any degree of certainty. One solution to the problem of getting the hole, the ball, and the eyes in a direct line was the shuffleboard putter. This came in a variety of forms, the favorite being a cylindrical head on a long shaft, up to eight feet in some cases. The technique was to place the clubhead on the turf behind the ball, take aim along that barrel of a shaft, and shove. It worked only too well, if not quite so effectively as a billiard cue, and the authorities duly ruled it out of court. Apart from offending against tradition, the shuffleboard putter could be indicted under Rule 19, which requires that "the ball must be fairly struck at with the head of the club and must not be pushed, scraped, or spooned."

The legal position was rather more moot

when the croquet putter came into fashion. The club conformed to the center-shafted specifications, and the stroke itself, swung between the legs with the player facing the hole, did not offend against Rule 19. Many golfers, especially those whose nerves had become worn to shreds through years of putting tension, found a new lease on golfing life through the croquet method. Sam Snead, the most notable exponent among the professionals, has achieved some success with croquet putting. Although it helped some golfers, croquet putting was not a superior method, per se. No great championship successes were achieved by the croquet brigade, nor were any putting records broken. It was different but demonstrably not better. The croquet

putter did not give its user an unfair advantage. All it did was to permit some golfers to compete on level terms again with conventional putters.

So, you may ask, why not leave well enough alone? The argument was persuasive—and advanced with great force and forensic skill at the time —but in the end the powers of tradition prevailed and croquet putting was banned. That is to say, rules were introduced forbidding a golfer to stand astride the line of his putt, and the specification of putter was altered to forbid the shaft to be sunk into the putter head exactly perpendicular. Sam Snead neatly got around the new regulations by facing the hole, as usual, but positioning himself beside the ball, instead of behind it. He

233

The American women's team of 1930, the year which saw the first unofficial match against Great Britain (later to become the biennial encounter for the Curtis Cup). Glenna Collett Vare is standing second from right.

called it his sidewinder style and found it no less effective than the old croquet method. Most of the other erstwhile croquet putters simply reverted to the conventional style. Although the authorities took a particularly ponderous steamhammer to crack this inconsequential nut, they were surely right to ban croquet putting. It most certainly was not golf. Above the tedious legal wrangling there remained the feeling that croquet putters were not playing the game as we had come to know it. The governing bodies are often criticized, and with justice, for their pettifogging legalistic attitudes, but in most cases they are motivated by a genuine desire to preserve the original forms of the game. Their instincts are sound, as they proved when they brought in the fourteen-club rule. Professionals were sponsored by manufacturers on the basis of the number of clubs they carried (or, to be accurate, their long-suffering caddies had to carry). Absurdity was achieved when pros had thirty clubs in the bag and the idea was spreading through the ranks of club players that such a complement of ironmongery was "necessary." Some believe that the maximum limit could well be lowered further to eleven or ten.

Weird and wonderful clubs by no means exhaust the inventive genius of golfers. Patent offices are stacked with designs for devices to make golfers play better. Enormous contraptions fitted with pulleys and clanking cogs have been built to educate a golfer's muscles to perform a geometrically perfect swing There is even a design for a pivoted tee from which the ball will be dispatched with magically induced extra energy.

The ball has not been neglected. Every possible variety of filling for the inner core has been tried, including porridge, with subsequent claims of almost supernatural qualities. Alas for us golfers, the main thrust of inventive energy in the field of golf equipment has been directed toward marketing and advertising. Very little valid scientific research has

World premier women's championship, the U.S. Women's Open—here at Winged Foot, 1972. Lower pictures show a few of the stars of the distaff circuit; left to right: Althea Gibson Darben, Betsy Rawls, Kathy Cornelius, Judy Rankin.

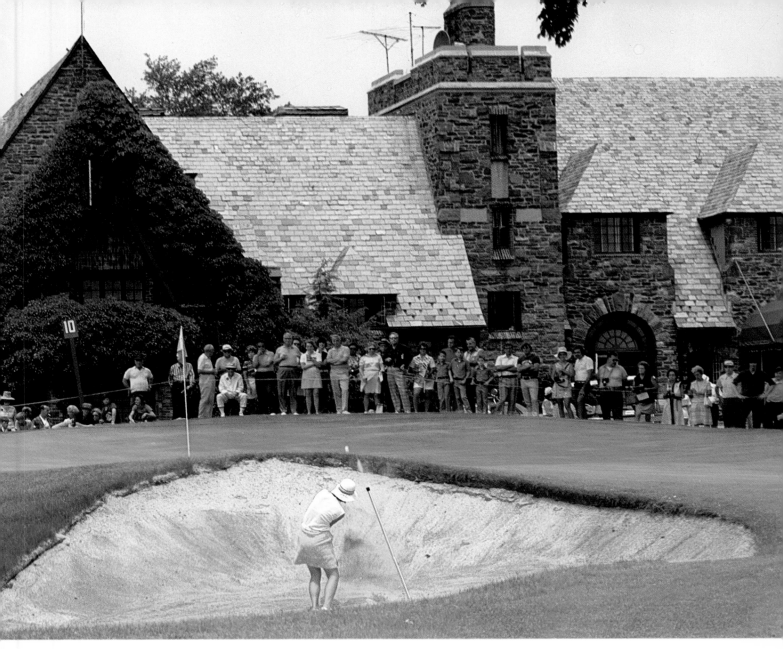

1

2

5

6

7

gone into golf. Those studies which have been undertaken suggest, indeed prove in some cases, that many of the accepted theories about the properties of golf clubs are scientifically unsound. Yet the makers continue in their old ways, preferring to employ a copywriter who can turn out effective scientific mumbo jumbo for their ads, rather than put a scientist to work to improve the product. It is all very sad, knowing that technical improvements could be made in our equipment, but at the same time it must be admitted that the most important quality a club can possess is the faith of the man who swings it.

The Irish professional Jimmy Kinsella hammered a second shaft inside the shaft of his driver. Scientifically, the idea is absurd. As Bobby Jones wisely observed, the shaft simply connects the hands with the clubhead and of itself imparts nothing to the shot. Of course it doesn't. It is nothing but dead weight. Yet because Kinsella believes in his double-shafted driver it works for him in the same way that Roberto de Vi-

cenzo can play well only with a ball marked with a "4." A surprising number of golfers are victims of such superstitions. Some have lucky colors. Others perform odd rituals like kissing their putters before every putt. (Bobby Locke actually slept with his, but that was more to ensure that no one stole the precious wand than to keep it in a good mood.) Nearly every tournament pro likes to follow a set routine, which seems sensible enough until you realize that these preliminaries often include such irrational details as insisting on putting on the left shoe first. It is all harmless enough most of the time, but if circumstances arise to upset the *idée fixe*, then the golfer can be undone. If that lucky sweater is lost so is the player.

Occasionally superstitions produce ludicrous situations, as in a mixed-foursome competition some years ago. A woman had got into the habit of teeing her ball right up against the tee marker, within three inches of it. The habit began as an aid to break her tendency to an exaggerated in-to-out swing. The

Cartoonist Charles Saxon's view of golf. The comedy is not greatly exaggerated—such incidents are not unknown on the course, although usually the salvage operation is to recover prosaic item such as car keys.

arrangement made her swing along the line of the shot, and it got so that she had to have the tee marker right by the ball whenever she used her driver. This time, aware of the crowd watching and playing with a famous partner, she was naturally nervous, and she missed the ball completely. So the next shot had to be played by her partner. That tee marker would have been disturbing enough to any golfer, but in this case it was worse because he was left-handed. All he could do was make a token pass which counted technically as another air shot so that she could have another go. The woman made contact on her second attempt but it was not much of a shot.

No golf club is complete without a reproduction of a portrait showing an early golfer in his splendid uniform of scarlet jacket. In our enlightened way we tend to find the thought of a uniform for golf slightly amusing. "Fancy getting yourself up in an outfit like that to play golf" we tell each other, without realizing that we ourselves are hardly less given to

peacock finery on the links. Those old golfers inherited the tradition of uniforms from the archery societies whose colorful coats performed the same valuable function as the red jackets which modern hunters are encouraged to wear. They identified the wearers and saved them from being shot at and did likewise for golfers. Even today on one London muncipal course in a deer park, the patrons have to wear red shirts or sweaters.

However, the impulse to dress up, and thereby make leisure activities more enjoyable, is a basic human instinct. The only special article of dress we actually need for playing golf is a pair of studded shoes, and even then a player who is properly balanced does not require anything like the full set of destructive studs of a modern golf shoe. (The studding pattern of golf shoes is one area which has been neglected by researchers. Yet if the teachers of golf are to be believed, a right shoe with studs only under the ball of the foot and the inside of the sole ought to ensure

Preceding pages: Results of human ingenuity to simplify
golf, all illegal and often misguided, include toothed water-mashie,
streamlined driver (bottom), and putter with aiming device.
Above: Contentious 6/100th difference, British and American balls.

correct leg action. And any arrangement which reduced the number of studs would be a boon to greenkeepers. In a four-day tournament over a million studs pierce the surface of greens and make putting difficult in the closing stages.)

Yet we sheeplike creatures wear special clothing for our game, and what is more we allow ourselves to be persuaded that the trademark on a golf shirt affects our game. Today's golfer believes that by buying clubs with Arnold Palmer's name stamped on them he is purchasing some degree of his skill. The assumptions in this subconscious train of thought are too foolish to enumerate, but the effect is a powerful marketing force. In the same way, but even more absurdly, Billy Casper shirts, Lee Trevino hats, and Gary Player slacks are jujus to us sophisticated golfers. Protest as we may to the contrary, the idea of reserving special clothes for golf proves that at best we are sheep following the flock and at worst we are superstitious sheep who imagine that we are turning ourselves into tigers.

When there is no advantage to be found in clothing or equipment, there is always the leverage inherent in a judiciously offered bet. The tradition of having a little "interest" on the side must be nearly as old as golf itself; in moderation a little flutter is harmless enough. As to what constitutes "little," this depends. The safe rule is never to gamble for more than you can afford to lose without flinching. As soon as a golfer goes in over his head he can be quite sure that his game will suffer. The hustlers know this and use their knowledge to advantage. And there are more than a few unscrupulous characters about, mainly operating resort courses, who are all too anxious to take the unsuspecting golfer for his roll.

The usual American convention is the nassau, which means three bets: one on the first nine holes, one on the second nine, and one on the match. A $10 nassau thus involves a total liability of $30. In addition, there is the four-ball system of corners, $10 a corner on the match. Here the novice should establish clearly what is meant. Usage varies. Sometimes a $10 corner is taken to mean that each of the two losers pays $10 to both winners. Sometimes it is taken to involve a total liability of $10 from the losing side to be shared by the winning pair. More correctly, this is a bet of $10 a side, but it is good to be sure of the liability before the match starts. For match play there is the extra complication of the press bet. That is, when one player (or pair) falls two holes behind he can "press," start a new match on the remaining holes for half the stake (as well as continuing the main bet, of course). Further complications arise over byes. When a match is finished, say by four and three, the remaining three holes can be played as a separate match, or bye. Thus it is possible to get a complexity of bets going at once, with the match and its bye, the first press and its bye, and the second press and its bye, and so on. Few golfers have the mental agility to keep track of all these transactions and the safe rule is to note all the scores and bets on the card for a grand reckoning at the end. But what sounds like a straightforward $10 match can easily involve $100 changing hands, so it is wise to be wary.

On the subject of hustling, even greater caution is required. Hustlers usually operate singly, although they occasionally hunt in pairs. A golfer on vacation is the favorite quarry and the operation normally begins with an affable invitation for a game with a small stake. The object is to assess the quality of the opposition and to let the vacationer win. This is a process known as salting the pigeon and produces an obligation for a return match. This the vacationer is usually all too happy to provide. He may be allowed to win again, for a bit more interest. He is being set up, and once the psychological moment arrives there follows some casual remark such as, "I had a good night at the tables and I might as well lose it to you as give it all back to the roulette wheel. Shall we raise the ante?" It is at this point that the wise vacationer suddenly develops a chronic attack of rheumatism.

The madness of golfers takes two general forms. There are the idiosyncrasies the player brings with him when he takes up the game; the irrational examples we have been discussing fall mostly into that category. Then there is the rather more insidious form of disorder which comes from long exposure to the mind-bending game itself.

For instance, take the singular experiment of the three golf balls and the effect it had on its victims. At the time when the USGA and the R. and A. were pondering the possibility of a uniform golf ball for all the world, a number of examples of the suggested compromise ball fell into the hands of an evil newspaper golf correspondent.* In the interests of the golfing public he took himself off to try out some of the new-size balls. After hitting several shots he began to think he was losing his reason. Being a Machiavellian fellow, he thought that rather then send himself mad it would be vastly preferable to inflict this fate on the members of his club. He knew that, given a uniform shot, the small, British-size ball 1.62 inches in diameter would go farther than the 1.68-inch American ball and that the medium-sized compromise ball of 1.66 inches would perform somewhere between the two extremes. And this is exactly what happened, in accordance with the immutable laws of dynamics.

However, when he collected up all the balls and threw them down in haphazard fashion, there were instances when he could not distinguish which balls were which. When that happened, and he did not know the size of the ball he was hitting, the results changed. There was no pattern to the shots. Some of the big balls went just as far as the small ones, and vice versa. The middle-size balls' behavior was similarly capricious. The cynic will say that the explanation was simple: He was a lousy golfer who couldn't hit a consistent shot and, as a matter of fact, the cynic would be right. But why, in that case, did the small ball go farther in the first experiment? A number of club members were summoned, some of them players of no mean skill. Just to make sure, the pro was included among the guinea pigs. The same thing happened. When they did not know which ball was which, the golfers performed much the same with every shot. Some went farther than others but the outcome was entirely random without any relationship between distance and the size of the ball. Yet when they tried again, this time being told which ball was which, the results conformed almost exactly with expectations. Disregarding obvious mis-hits, the small ball outdistanced the 1.66, and the big ball came last. (The exception to that norm was the pro who, knowing the ball sizes, hit the big one consistently farther than the other two sizes. He explained that since he always played the big ball—as required by the British PGA—he had developed a technique which was especially suited to it.) The effect on the ordinary players can be imagined. Believing for years that their small ball gave them 15 yards extra on their drives, they now had proof that notwithstanding the laws of nature they played just as well with the 1.66 or the 1.68. In fact, the size of the ball had the same significance for practical purpose as the number 4 painted on Roberto de Vicenzo's ball.

Even more traumatic experiences await the golfer. Nongolfers are frequently puzzled by the extraordinary rituals which pros perform as they face up to a 3-foot putt. "Why is he going through that song and dance over that tiddler? Why I could knock it in with one hand."

And so he could, once or twice, or maybe ten times. Then he would miss one and his troubles would start. For the pro the importance of the occasion makes the difference. Apart from that, golfers acquire a personal case history of disaster which can affect them almost as strongly as a physical jog on the elbow

* The author.

at the critical moment. Imagine the residual damage caused by Walter Hagen's experience of twitching a putt out-of-bounds, which itself may have been the result of past disasters.

Brian Barnes, the British Ryder Cup player, was in contention for the French Open at Saint-Cloud in 1968 and was going well when he came to the 8th hole in the second round. It is a par-3, and a short one at that, with no special difficulties. Barnes bunkered his tee shot and his recovery left him a long putt. Still smarting at his poor recovery, Barnes proved again the old saying that an angry man never hit a good shot. His approach putt was 3 feet short and with that old red curtain coming up over his eyes he lipped out the 3-footer. He raked at the ball and missed and by now he was lost. He patted the ball to and fro and by the time it dropped, what with penalty strokes for hitting a moving ball and standing astride his line, his playing partners reckoned him to be down in 15. Not surprisingly Barnes made a hurried exit from the scene. Who can tell what scars that experience left on his subconscious long after the incident was forgotten?

Tommy Armour was just one golfer who allowed his stubbornness to get the better of him. The week after he won the U.S. Open he was feeling that he could make the ball do anything he liked. He came to the 17th hole of the Shawnee Open and decided that the best way to play was to hit a long draw off the tee. The difference between a draw and a hook is, all too often, the out-of-bounds fence and that's just what happened. Armour was determined to play that draw shot and fired away off the tee, only to see ball after ball soar over the fence. His card was marked with a 21 for the hole, but afterward Armour disputed the figure. He insisted it should have been 23. It just proves once again that golf cannot be conquered.

After a lifetime of daily application, the game still has the power to turn and rend the complacent golfer. In realistic terms the game of golf defies success. Over some forty years, that is to say something like twenty thousand rounds by the world's most accomplished players, the ringer score, or eclectic, for the best eighteen holes at Augusta in the Masters is 38 strokes. Potentially that figure could be reduced by four more shots and doubtless will be in time, as players have the luck to hole out with approach shots. We can say, then, that a score of 34 would represent perfection at Augusta. The course record is 64, which demonstrates that the finest golf by the world's best players is a long, long way from perfect. We are all doomed to failure when we take a golf club in hand. The height of anyone's ambition can only be that his failures be modest. And it is here, surely, that can be found both the source of golf's lunacy and its sanity.

Almost everything in golf is a paradox. The learner discovers through distracted trial and error that in order to make a ball go upward it must be hit downward, and that if the ball is to be hit far it must be struck with a slow swing. At every turn in the game these paradoxes occur. We tell ourselves that golf is a microcosm of life itself, but in truth it is life through the looking glass, life in paradox. And so we come to the comforting thought that the madness which manifests itself in every golfer is really, in our back-to-front world, quite normal. The man who devoted an entire room as a shrine to Arnold Palmer becomes by this interpretation entirely rational, as does the man who has created a large lawn from collected divots torn from golf courses by the clubs of the stars.

By the same token we who shoulder our clubs and seek to master what we know can never be mastered, are perhaps not so irrational as we sometimes fear. For what we are doing is to chase the bitch-goddess Failure. That is golf's ultimate paradox and it could be that we only appear mad from the other side of the looking glass. Maybe we are really the sane ones. And if not, never mind. Golf is fun and that, when you get right down to it, is all that matters.

243

photo credits

index

Caption references in italics

a

Acquasanta (Italy), *110*
Africa, golf in, *112*, 128
Alcan tournament, 90–94
American swing, 178
Anderson, Willie, 203
Apple-Tree Gang, 69, *71*
Archer, George, 178
Armour, Tommy, 169, 197, 243
Arnie's Army, 99–101
Auchterlonie, Lawrence, 203
Augusta National Golf Club, *118,*
    139–140, *141*, 148–149,
    154, 211–213, 243
Australia, golf in, 99, 143–144, 230
Ayrshire, 81
Ayton, David, 196

b

Baffing spoon, 49, 53
Ball(s), 48–49, 50, 64, 65, 129
    featherie, 48, *62*
    gutta-percha, *62*, 64–65
    Haskell, *62*, 65
    variations in size, *240*, 242
Ball, John, 220
Ballybunion, 149
Baltusrol, *60*, 133
Banff, 109
Barnes, Brian, 243
Barnes, Jim, 197
Bemidji (Minn.), *29*
Bendelow, Tom, 75
Berg, Patty, 185
Betting, 241–242
Big Three, 188
Birkdale, *see* Royal Birkdale
Boros, Julius, 28, 210
Bradshaw, Harry, 198, 200
Brady, Mike, 205
Braid, James, 162, *167*, 169, 197
Brassie, 53

Briggs, Clare, *20*
British Amateur championship, 78
    (1904), 152–153 (1930), *161*
    (1930), *198* (1886), 220, 232 (1904)
British Open championship,
    25 (1926), 65, 82, 87, 128 (1971),
    136 (1968), 144 (1972), *144*
    (1969), 149 (1970), 152 (1930), 153
    (1930), 157, 166, 168, 169, *178*
    (1928), 192 (1971), 200
    (1951, 1953), 196–203 (history),
    197 (1914, 1926), 198 (1934,
    1937, 1947, 1950), 201 (1953), *201*
    (1937, 1965), 203 (1961, 1962),
    209 (1969), 217 (1971), 228 (1965)
Brookline, *88*, 205
Browning, Robert, 37, 69
Bye, 241

c

Caddy(ies), 58, *79*, 167
Campbell, Willie, 203
Capilano (B.C.), 109
Carnoustie, 136, 144, 169, 198, 201
Carter, Ed, 96
Casper, Billy, 174, *188, 206*
Castle Harbour (Bermuda), *110*
Castletroy, *123*
Championships, development of, 64
Charles, Bob, 187–188
Chole, 36–37, *38, 43*
Cleek, 53
Clubs, golf, 44, 49–50, 51–53, 65, *154*
    distance vs. accuracy, 193
    early, 44, 49–50, 53, *152, 154*
    hickory, 172
    illegal, 232, *240*
    limitation of number, 234
    steel, *1*72
    women's, 232
    see also clubs by name
Coles, Neil, *96*
Cornelius, Kathy, *234*
Corners (betting), 241

Cotton, Henry, 173, *180*, 198, *201*
Courses, golf, 53, 108, 113–114, 124
    architecture of, 132–149
Crans-sur-Sierre, 109, *110*
Crosby, Bing, 139
Crosse, 37
Curtis Cup, *222*
Cypress Point, 137–139, *196*

d

Daly, Fred, 198
Danecki, Walter, 228
Darben, Althea Gibson, *234*
Demaret, Jimmy, *183*
Desert golf, 108–109
De Vicenzo, Roberto, 187, 217, 236–237
Dey, Joe, 220
Driving ranges (Japan), 121
Dudley, Ed, 198
Dunn, Willie, 203
Dutra, Olin, 210

e

Earnings, 225
Edinburgh Golfers, Honourable
    Society of, 196
El Conquistador (P.R.), 26

f

Faulkner, Max, 200
Feather(ie) ball, 48, *62*
Fife, 81, 121
Foulis, James, 203
France, golf in, 114

g

Gambling, 128, 241–242
Geared, Bob, 229